For Love of Money

FOR LOVE OF MONEY

Sixteen Murders for Gain

GEORGINA LLOYD

ROBERT HALE · LONDON

Robert Hale Limited
Clerkenwell House
Clerkenwell Green
London EC1R 0HT

ISBN 0–7090–4390–8

Photoset in North Wales by
Derek Doyle & Associates, Mold, Clwyd.
Printed in Great Britain by
St Edmundsbury Press, Bury St Edmunds, Suffolk.
Bound by WBC Bookbinders Limited, Bridgend, Glamorgan.

Contents

Introduction

In a sense, all murder is for gain. If the killer is not murdering for money, then he (or she) is killing to gain control over another person, or control over a situation. The man who kills his wife so that he can marry a mistress is a case in point. So, too, in a more indirect context, is a man who inadvertently kills another man in a frenzy of rage, sparked off by an insult. In this case he has attempted to gain control over the other man's offensive behaviour by stopping it with a disabling blow; the fact that the blow happened to be lethal is by the way.

In this book, however, we are going to look at cases in which the murderer deliberately killed for monetary gain. Although statistically not the commonest motive for murder, it is one which, however odious, can at least be easily understood. Many murders are committed for more obscure motives which sometimes need unravelling by a psychiatrist; this is especially true in the case of, for instance, psychopathic murderers. Examples include a serial murderer who killed only long-haired blondes, because these girls symbolized the long-haired blonde who had jilted him; similarly, a man who hated his mother killed several women who closely resembled her. He did not kill his mother because, in his own words, 'I could not bring myself to do it' – which, the psychiatrists averred, was a form of subconscious sexual love which was masquerading as hatred – the Oedipus complex. His subconscious guilt at his incestuous feelings forced him symbolically to destroy its cause.

By comparison, murder for monetary gain is simple and straightforward – there are no obscure subconscious

7

motives here. Lust for lucre, greed for gold, madness for money – call it what you will, it is a motive almost as old as man himself. The murderer is simply envious of another's wealth or possessions, and if the only way to secure it is to kill, then that is what he sets out to do, by devious means such as poison, or more direct means such as shooting, stabbing or strangling.

The method used to kill reflects the character of the murderer to a great extent. The quiet, introverted person is more likely to use a quiet, inconspicuous method such as slow poisoning, although this is not necessarily always true. Women also seem to prefer this method; it is quite rare for a woman to stab or strangle, though there have of course been exceptions. Shooting seems to be favoured by both men and women if the circumstances are propitious for such an overt method to be used with – according to the killer's thinking – not much likelihood of being found out.

This book documents a variety of such cases. In some of them the stakes played for have been high, running into thousands of pounds, or dollars or whatever; in others the gain has been pitifully meagre, in some cases only shillings. But the motive has been the same – destroying the life of the person who owned the money in order to obtain it – in other words, for the killer to gain control of another's property.

Georgina Lloyd
October 1990

1

A Piece of Cake

Dr George Henry Lamson (1882)

A doctor, by the very nature of his profession, is conversant with dangerous drugs, and usually keeps a supply of various medicines and chemicals in his surgery, many of which, although they have beneficial uses in knowledgeable hands, are deadly poisons if misused. Fortunately for the rest of mankind, the vast majority of doctors are responsible individuals who combine the desire to alleviate the sufferings of their fellow men and women with the perfectly normal desire to earn a decent living in the profession of their choice.

However, in almost every profession there is the exception that proves the rule: the 'black sheep' who brings the honour of his calling into disrepute. Particularly odious is the doctor who abuses the trust his position invites by exploiting his access to, and knowledge of, deadly poisons in order to kill his fellow human beings for gain. Such a one was Dr George Henry Lamson, the son of a Church of England clergyman, who practised in the 1880s.

It was at about this time, in 1879 to be precise, that Lamson met a Miss John, one of the four surviving children of a comfortably off family in which both parents had died at an early age. The children, being under age, became wards in Chancery and were put under the guardianship of various relatives; the youngest son, Percy Malcolm John, was the ward of a Mr Chapman, who had married his eldest sister after she came of age. Percy was crippled from birth and confined to a wheelchair, and was being educated at Blenheim House School in Wimbledon. This was a boarding-school patronized by what in those days were referred to as the 'upper classes' and the pupils included the sons of some titled persons, high-ranking government officials, and so on.

When Lamson married the younger of the two sisters in the John family, he became entitled to her share of the small fortune left to her by her parents. The Married Women's Property Act had not yet been passed, and her capital thus passed automatically into the possession of her husband. The new Mrs Lamson had no apparent objections to this state of affairs, and it appears that she was only too pleased to be in a position to help her husband who at the time was looking for a suitable practice to purchase, having recently qualified as an MD and an LRCP.

While thus engaged, his wife's brother Herbert died in what were later described as 'mysterious circumstances', and on his demise Mrs Lamson became entitled to a reversionary interest in his residuary estate, amounting to something between seven and eight hundred pounds in government stocks and shares. This now came into Lamson's possession, while similar amounts devolved to Mrs Chapman and the young Percy John. If Percy (now eighteen) were to live until he came of age (or, to use the legal phraseology of the documents involved, attained his majority, which in those days was twenty-one) he would succeed to some £3,000, but if he were to die in the meantime each of his surviving sisters (one of whom was, of course, Mrs Lamson) would receive a one-third share, amounting to about £1,500 or so. The husbands would, of course, have been entitled to their wives' share, as the law then stood.

The death of Herbert thus put a little more capital into Lamson's hands and early in the following year he purchased a practice in Bournemouth, where he appeared to be settling nicely, except for one thing: he gradually became addicted to morphine. Eventually his addiction to the drug had escalated to the point that he started to neglect his practice, so that by March 1881 he had lost most of his patients, writs and summonses were issued against him for debts, and he had to sell his home in Bournemouth. The BMA also struck him off their roll.

With what he managed to salvage from the wreckage, Lamson took ship for America, but there appears to be no record of what he did while there. Whatever it was, it proved so unsuccessful that by July of the same year he had booked a passage home, apparently working his passage by assisting the ship's medical officer instead of paying his fare. By the time the ship docked in Liverpool, Lamson was so impoverished that he borrowed £5 from a crew member before landing.

His wife was devoted to him and had faithfully stood by him through all his trials and tribulations, and now once again she did her best to support him as he cast around for another practice to purchase. This he found in Rotherfield, near Crowborough in Sussex, but he was stupid enough to have the name of a well-known Crowborough surgeon engraved on his brass name plate besides his own, entirely without permission. This gentleman was, not unreasonably, very annoyed, and publicly denounced Lamson as a cheat and an impostor. This so inflamed local feeling against Lamson that, only two months after he had purchased the practice, he was forced to put it up for sale. He sold it at a considerable loss, and once more set out for America, where he still hoped to amass a fortune, but again he was disappointed. Only a few weeks later he returned to Bournemouth.

He now decided to try his luck in London, and a retired surgeon in Bournemouth decided to help him by giving him his case of surgical instruments. On either 24 or 25 October he arrived in the capital and took up residence at Nelson's Hotel in Great Portland Street. London, however, proved as disappointing as America, and it seems that the bill for his stay at Nelson's Hotel could not be paid.

On 24 November the doctor pawned the case of surgical instruments and his gold watch and chain, obtaining only £5 for the lot. He then decided to descend, uninvited, on his sister and brother-in-law, the Chapmans, who lived on

the Isle of Wight. Their last known address was Ryde, but
when he arrived in that town he discovered that they had
moved to Ventnor. Not having enough money to pay the
fare, he applied to the stationmaster at Ryde to allow him
to travel without paying for his ticket on the understanding that Mr Chapman would pay at the other end. Mr
Chapman did so, but was so annoyed at the barefaced
effrontery of his brother-in-law in suddenly turning up
without any warning and imposing upon him in this way,
that he refused to put him up for the night or have
anything more to do with him. Lamson was therefore
once more thrown upon his own resources.

He managed to persuade a Mr Price Owen, a tradesman
in the High Street in Ventnor, to lend him £10 – which he
later increased to £20 – against a postdated cheque for £15.
Having obtained the loan, and knowing full well that this
cheque was not worth the paper it was written on,
Lamson hot-footed it back to London and re-established
residence at Nelson's Hotel. Before reaching London he
stopped along the way and sent the following telegram to
Price Owen:

JUST DISCOVERED THAT CHEQUE YOU ASKED FOR
YESTERDAY MADE ON WRONG BANK STOP PLEASE
DON'T SEND IT ON STOP LETTER FOLLOWS NEXT
POST STOP – LAMSON

That night he sent the promised letter, which was dated
1 December 1881:

Dear Sir,
    I sent you a telegram before leaving my friends at
Horsham telling you I had written my cheque on the
wrong bank, which was the case. I formerly had an
account with the Wilts and Dorset Bank but have since
transferred my business to another house. The cheques are
of the same colour, and as I was in a great rush to leave
home I grabbed from my desk drawer what I thought was
the right book, but I was mistaken. I had taken my old
Wilts and Dorset cheque book, which still contained a few
blank cheques. I have not the right book with me, but have
wired home for it to be sent to me by return ... and shall

then immediately set the matter right with you. Begging you will pardon such an excusable piece of stupidity on my part, I remain, dear Sir,

Yours faithfully,
George H. Lamson, MD

This missive certainly takes the biscuit for a devious ploy, and the sending of the letter from Horsham ('I have not the right book with me') was ingeniously thought out to disarm the gullible Price Owen who, it need scarcely be pointed out, waited in vain for the return of his loan. But there was a glaring discrepancy in this rigmarole, and anyone less gullible than its recipient would have seen through it for the con it was. Lamson had said that the cheques of the two banks were the same colour. While this might be so, it is unlikely that the two cheque books would have lain *open* in his desk drawer, and it is equally unlikely that the *covers* of the two books were identical.

The fact was that Lamson did still have an account with the Wilts and Dorset Bank, but he had been advised that his account was overdrawn and that no further cheques would be honoured. He had no account with any other bank – which was, perhaps, as well for the banks.

However, this did not stop Lamson from somehow obtaining a cheque slip from another bank, which he made out for the sum of £12 10s 0d; he then set about cashing it. Eventually he managed to persuade the landlord of the Eyre Arms, in St John's Wood, to cash the cheque for him. An overdraft at one's own bank is one thing, but to attempt to cash a cheque drawn on a bank with which one has no account, is a criminal offence. Lamson was treading on very thin ice indeed.

That same night he wrote to his brother-in-law Percy John at Blenheim House School:

My dear Percy,
I had intended … coming to see you at Wimbledon today, but have been delayed by various matters, and it is now nearly six o'clock and by the time I should reach Blenheim House you would probably be preparing for bed. I leave for Paris and Florence tomorrow and wish to see

you before going, so I purpose to see you as early as I can,
for a few minutes even if I can accomplish no more.
Believe me, dear boy,
Your loving brother,
G.H. Lamson.

The letter was undated, but was sent on 1 December, the
same day as the letter Lamson sent to Price Owen. He
had, it seems, already decided on the course of action
which he deemed to be the only way out of his financial
difficulties, for one week previously, on 24 November, he
had purchased two grains of aconitine, then a little-known
poison, from Messrs Allen and Hanbury, whose premises
at that time were in Plough Court, off Lombard Street, in
the City.

On 2 December Lamson, accompanied by a young
medical student named Tulloch with whom he had
become friendly, set out for Wimbledon. When they
arrived at the railway station Lamson told Tulloch to wait
for him there while he went off to pay his visit to his
brother-in-law. When he returned, after some considerable time, he told Tulloch that the boy 'was very ill and
getting worse', adding that he would postpone his trip to
France and Italy and visit Percy once more the following
day before leaving.

This was yet another of the doctor's devious ploys. He
had not been to Blenheim House; he had not seen Percy;
and Percy was in perfect health (apart from his disability, a
curvature of the spine which rendered him from birth
unable to walk.) It would seem that he was anxious that
Tulloch should gain the impression, just in case he were
ever asked about the matter, that Percy was ill *before*
Lamson's purported second visit to his brother-in-law ...

Lamson and Tulloch then returned, Tulloch to his
lodgings and Lamson to an unknown destination. The
doctor did not return to Nelson's Hotel that night, and it
was never discovered where he spent the night of 2
December 1881.

The following day Percy enjoyed the usual weekend
routine at his boarding-school. As it was a Saturday there

were no lessons, and he was able to indulge in his hobbies of reading (the school had a splendid library) and chess, as well as watching cricket. He had a wheelchair upstairs and another one downstairs, and other boys carried him about up or down the stairs as required. At seven o'clock Dr Lamson was announced, and Percy was wheeled into the headmaster's study to meet him and take tea with him. Mr Bedbrook, the head, was pleased to note that the boy's brother-in-law had made the journey to visit him before his avowed intention of leaving for the Continent on a business trip.

While Mr Bedbrook sent for tea for three, Lamson produced a Dundee cake which had already been portioned into three slices. As soon as the necessary plates were forthcoming, he transferred these slices on to them. The trio sat enjoying their tea and the Dundee cake so thoughtfully brought by their visitor, until the clock chimed a quarter past seven. Five minutes after this Dr Lamson announced that he had better be making a move as he had a train to catch if he were to reach Paris in time for the first of his business appointments. Mr Bedbrook pointed out that the doctor had already missed the first London to Paris train on the evening schedule and that he had plenty of time to catch the next one. But Dr Lamson insisted on leaving immediately, and the head saw him to the door, leaving Percy in the study.

Ten minutes after the doctor's departure, Percy began to feel – as he put it – 'a bit peculiar'. The headmaster rang for a couple of boys to carry Percy up to the school sick-room, and called the school's resident nurse. The boy had barely made it to the sick-room before vomiting, after which he started sweating and trembling and was seized with violent convulsions. He was laid fully clothed on the bed, the two boys who had carried him upstairs holding his limbs to prevent him from throwing himself off the bed on to the floor. The nurse became so alarmed that she sent for the school's doctor, a Dr Little, and his assistant, Dr Berry. The matron, Mrs Bowles, was also summoned, as well as one of the junior masters, named Goddard. The boy's symptoms became more intense, and the doctors said that they appeared to be consistent with food poisoning, though they wondered how this could have come about, since the boy had eaten only the same foods as all the other pupils and no one else was affected. The headmaster mentioned that he, Percy and their visitor had partaken of tea and cake; both he and the visitor had eaten the cake and drunk the tea, but only Percy had been taken ill. Dr Berry had the presence of mind to retain some of the patient's vomit in a basin for subsequent analysis.

The boy rapidly worsened, and the two doctors now concentrated their energies on attempting to relieve his sufferings with morphia. Percy went into a coma, and at about eleven o'clock that same night he died. Mr Bedbrook, understandably, did not wish to call the police until the following morning, and when he did so he asked Inspector Fuller, who took charge of the case, that as little publicity as possible be given to the school to preserve its good reputation.

A post-mortem, and an analysis of the vomit preserved in the basin, showed that some kind of vegetable alkaloid poison, of unknown identity or origin, had been administered. So far, no one had considered the Dundee cake provided by Dr Lamson, but now it appeared that the poison had been injected into the raisins in the piece of cake which had been handed to Percy John. Suspicion, of course, attached to Dr Lamson, but no one could question him because he had hurriedly left the country, and that was suspicious in itself. His alleged 'business appointments' in Paris and Florence were, no doubt, a fake. How to apprehend him if no one knew his exact whereabouts?

Fate now took a hand in the shape of the suspect himself, who suddenly and without warning presented himself at Scotland Yard, on 8 December, although no warrant had been issued for his arrest, or appeal made for him to come forward. With the inexplicable urge that some murderers seem to have to bring themselves to the notice of the police of their own accord, he had come unbidden.

Lamson, at Scotland Yard, was seen by Inspector Butcher, who was considerably surprised to learn the identity of his visitor. 'I am Dr Lamson,' he announced, 'whose name has been mentioned in connection with the death at Wimbledon. I have called to see what is to be done about it; I considered it best to do so, as I read the account in the papers in Paris and came over this morning – I have only just arrived in London ...'

Shades of Neville George Clevely Heath ('I have called in to see if I can help you clear up any misunderstanding'), John George Haigh ('I've come to see if there is anything I can do to clear up this mystery') and Buck Ruxton who kept going to see the police to tell them to stop hounding him! All three walked voluntarily into a police station, some more than once, and all three kept an appointment with the hangman.

Inspector Butcher, confronted by Lamson, felt rather out of his depth. He sent for Superintendent Williamson, who told Lamson that 'he would have to remain for a time' while he obtained information from his superiors. Lamson was left with Inspector Butcher, with whom it appeared that he had a pleasant chat on general topics. It would seem that this conversation lasted some considerable time, because it is on record that Lamson at last became restive and asked why there was such a delay, as he intended to leave for the country. He asked if he might leave his address where the police could contact him if necessary, and stated that he would attend the inquest.

Inspector Butcher went to find Williamson and obtain instructions from him. When he returned, he asked Dr Lamson to accompany him into another room, where Superintendent Williamson now formally addressed him: 'Dr Lamson, this case has been fully considered, and it has been decided to charge you with causing the death. I therefore take you into custody and charge you with causing the death of Percy Malcolm John at Blenheim House, Wimbledon, on 3 December 1881.'

Lamson replied, 'Very well', with a calm that he must have been far from feeling. Then he added, 'Do you think they would accept bail? I hope the matter will be kept as quiet as possible, for the sake of my relations.' Williamson replied that he would be taken to Wandsworth police station, and that the question of bail would rest with the magistrates.

Williamson accompanied his charge in a cab to Wandsworth, there being no fast squad cars in those days. During the journey Lamson remarked that his father would arrive in a day or two, and added, 'I hope it will be stated that I came to Scotland Yard of my own free will. I came from Paris on purpose.' To this, Williamson replied, 'Certainly.'

*   *   *

The trial of Dr Lamson opened at the Old Bailey on Wednesday, 8 March 1882. The court was crowded to capacity, and the streets outside were thronged with the multitudes who had been unable to gain admission.

The judge was Mr Justice Hawkins; the prosecution was headed by the Solicitor General, Sir F. Herschel, assisted by Mr Poland and Mr Gladstone (no relation to the famous Prime Minister), and Lamson was defended by Mr Montague Williams, Mr Charles Mathews (later to become Public Prosecutor) and Mr W.S. Robson.

The prosecution had a strong case, despite the fact that it was based almost entirely on circumstantial evidence. It was so completely documented, from the purchase of aconitine from Messrs Allen and Hanbury's a week before the murder, to its actual administration, via a piece of cake, in the headmaster's study, to the unsuspecting victim, that the outcome of the trial was scarcely in doubt. It also transpired that, prior to the purchase of the poison from Messrs Allen and Hanbury's, Lamson had attempted, unsuccessfully, to purchase aconitine from another chemist.

Another damning point against the accused was the production of a notebook which he had kept detailing various poisons and the effects they had on the human body. In this book, aconitine and its effects were described, the symptoms exactly similar to those suffered by the unfortunate Percy John. An asterisk was inscribed beside the heading 'Aconitine – a vegetable alkaloid' and at the end of its description the words 'Very suitable' had been appended in pencil.

'Very suitable for what?' thundered the Solicitor General. 'For murdering his brother-in-law for his inheritance!'

The defence had a difficult time trying to rebut these telling points. Would a murderer openly purchase poison in his own name? And would he openly administer the poison in the presence of a third party? Surely not. Mr Montague Williams, for all his mastery of powerful rhetoric, could not stem the tide of fatal evidence which had piled up, and he knew that he was on a losing wicket. Lamson himself, immaculately dressed and calm in the dock, felt his optimism waning, although he did not let it show. The judge's summing-up did nothing to reinforce what little hope he may still have had, and at six o'clock the jury retired. They needed but little time to come to a unanimous verdict of guilty. Only then did Lamson's composure visibly desert him. His face grew ashen, and he swayed unsteadily, supported on either side by a prison guard, as the judge asked him whether he had anything to say before the sentence was passed. 'I merely protest my innocence before God,' he replied.

He was transported to Wandsworth Prison, and the date fixed for his execution on 2 April, but it was not to take place on that date because of petitions which were set afoot for his reprieve. So unremitting were the efforts of his friends on his behalf that others in America joined them, and the President of the United States cabled the Home Secretary – an unprecedented step – for a postponement of the execution until various affidavits might be re-examined. Sir William Harcourt, the Home Secretary, agreed to this, but in the end it gained Lamson only a further twenty-six days of the half-life of a broken man in prison, for nothing was discovered in the affidavits sufficient to stay the course of the law. Lamson went to meet his Maker on 28 April 1882 at the hands of William Marwood, the public hangman.

2

London's Bonnie and Clyde

Karl Gustav Hulten and Elizabeth Jones (1945)

Wartime does strange things to young girls. The grim reality of war becomes invested with a spurious glamour. Fascinated by uniforms, a young girl who is not old enough to join the women's services (or who cannot obtain her parents' permission) will do the next best thing – associate with soldiers. Sometimes a girl will marry her soldier boyfriend and they will live happily ever after; in other cases, however, there is no such happy ending and disaster results. Elizabeth Jones was such a girl, and her association with an American GI – often the target of young girls in wartime – ended in murder.

Elizabeth Jones (who was known as Betty) was born in a tiny Welsh village. She was barely thirteen years of age when she decided that village life was boring and uneventful, and thought that the best thing to do would be to run away from home. She had not hitch-hiked very far when she was spotted and brought unceremoniously back by the police. In her school uniform, with her few belongings on her back, using her school satchel as a rucksack, she stood out like a sore thumb.

Undaunted by this experience, Betty made another attempt. This time she wore ordinary clothes and carried a shopping bag instead of her satchel. She got as far as Cardiff before being apprehended because she tried to board a bus without any money. Unable to pay her fare, the lame excuses she offered were not believed and she was bundled into the bus depot manager's office to await the arrival of the police.

At home she received a good talking-to, which did little good – it was like water off a duck's back. She pretended to conform to her family's admonishings, all the time planning her next attempt. This ended in similar fashion to the previous ones, and she gave up the idea as a bad job. She would work out some other ploy to gain the independence she so desperately longed for.

It was 1943. Her father had enlisted for the Army and what little control he had over his wayward daughter was now non-existent; her mother was too busy trying to keep the family together to be able to have very much influence on her. Soldiers were being billeted in the village, and Betty lost no time in chatting them up. Soon she found a young army private who wanted to marry her, and she jumped at this opportunity to gain the independence from her family that she craved. Although barely sixteen, Betty had no difficulty in getting her parents' permission for the wedding. The boy, they thought, was a nice enough lad, three years older than his bride, and they thought that marriage would encourage their wilful child to settle down.

Unfortunately, the idyll was destined to be short-lived. After the wedding in the chapel, the reception and the send-off on honeymoon, less than twenty-four hours later Betty was back in the parental home, to the astonishment of her parents, brothers and sisters and friends. On her wedding night her new husband had struck her, whereupon she left him without more ado. It is not known what the dispute was about. Her parents shook their heads in disbelief. Such a nice lad, they said – who would have imagined he would do a thing like that? The marriage was unconsummated and was annulled in due course.

In February 1943, just six weeks after the disastrous marriage, Betty finally cut loose from her family and set out for London. She now drew her husband's army allowance of £1 15s 6d a week (equivalent to £1.78 today) and augmented this by taking various jobs, mostly as a barmaid.

Betty's craving for excitement had never abated, and

she soon found it in the dance-halls, which were about as far from a Saturday-night hop in a Welsh village as you could get. She met plenty of men in uniform, her favourites being the American GIs with their free-spending habits and their tales of far-off America. Competition for these soldiers among the girls who attended the dance-halls was stiff, but Betty had two great advantages – a fabulous figure and exceptional good looks. Added to these assets was her lilting Welsh accent, which fascinated those unused to its cadences.

One of these Americans Betty met as a dancing partner had had some theatrical experience in civilian life before the war, and he taught her some simple routines and told her that she could easily, with her face and figure, earn a living on the stage. Betty took him at his word. She danced as much as she could and practised the routines in private, and within two months she was able to give up her boring job pulling pints in a pub and get a job as a striptease dancer in a night club. Here she was able to meet far more men, although she passed up the civilians and went out only with uniformed men, mainly Americans. One of these, a private in the US Army named Leonard Bexley, introduced her to another soldier, whose name was Karl Gustav Hulten, a 22-year-old paratrooper attached to an infantry regiment. One should, perhaps, say that he had been attached, for he was now in fact a deserter.

Hulten was using the name Ricky Allen while he was AWOL. He made no secret of the fact that he was a deserter – in fact he seemed to brag about it. Betty was immediately attracted to him, but it was not just on account of his blond good looks that he had inherited from his Scandinavian forebears. He exuded an air of bravado, a sort of swaggering defiance of authority, and it was this that evoked an answering chord in Betty's personality. She fell in love with him at first sight, and it was her undoing ... and his.

The couple spent all their free time together. He had the use of an army truck and used this as a private car. The two would drive around most of the time when Betty was not dancing at the night club. Ricky would go and watch her performance several nights a week.

One night, on Betty's night off, the couple were riding around in the truck. 'I bet you nicked this truck,' she said.

'You're dead right, baby,' he replied. 'If I want something, I just take it.'

Betty was thrilled by the way he called her 'baby', just like in the movies. 'You know what?' she said. 'I wish you were a real gangster! Then I could be a gangster's moll!'

'Yeah?' He looked hard at her. 'Well, now, I guess I could be a gangster, and you could be my moll. What shall we do? Rob somebody?'

'Yes! Let's go and rob somebody!' Betty enthused. 'Just so long as we don't get caught and end up in jail!'

Thus started a series of armed robberies – for Ricky had a gun. Betty gazed at it in a kind of horrified fascination. 'We won't kill anybody, will we?' she queried. 'Not unless we have to,' came the reply.

The first robbery was of a girl driving a large van. The army truck swung in front of her and pulled over, effectively blocking her path on a deserted suburban road. Betty climbed into the vehicle and pushed the girl out on the road. The following quotation is from Hulten's statement made after he was in custody.

> I caught her [the girl driver] and hit her over the head with an iron bar. She didn't fall down. I grabbed her round the neck and we both fell to the ground. She fell on her stomach, and I knelt on her back with my left leg on the ground. My right arm was around her and I told Betty to hold her arm. Betty knelt on her right arm and went through her coat pockets. As I recall, she found about five shillings. By this time the girl had stopped struggling. I picked her up by the shoulders and Betty lifted her feet. We carried her over, and dumped her about a yard from the edge of a stream. I threw the iron pipe into the stream. The girl's suitcase and handbag were left in the van.

The girl recovered consciousness in hospital, where she had been taken after being found by two boys out walking their dog. Her head wound required nine stitches, and she was off work for five weeks, all for the princely sum of five shillings. That's just 25p in present-day money. Some gangster – some moll!

Another victim – also a girl – was hauled bodily from her car at gunpoint, hit on the head with another length of iron piping and robbed of her identity card, food ration book, clothing coupons and about ten pounds in cash. She was then thrown into the Thames to drown. Fortunately she escaped with her life, though only by a lucky chance. A man had been doing a spot of night fishing from a bridge, and saw the whole thing. He dropped his rod and dived into the water to bring the victim to the bank, where he applied artificial respiration and sent a passer-by to ring for the police and an ambulance. He told police that he had been able to make out a large army truck which had roared off at speed after the attack, but since it had been dark he could not see the licence number.

Further robberies ensued, and London's wartime Bonnie and Clyde ran some incredible risks but were never apprehended. Their luck – if one can call it that – held until one night when Nemesis overtook them ...

* * *

On the morning of 7 October 1944 an auxiliary fireman happened to cross Knowle Green on the outskirts of Staines, Middlesex, when he came upon the body of a man lying in a ditch. He called the police.

It was quickly established that there was no money or anything else in the dead man's pockets, nor a watch, rings or other valuables. A bullet hole in his back and an exit wound in his chest indicated that he had been shot in the back – a finding confirmed by the subsequent autopsy.

About an hour earlier a workman walking along the Great South-west Road, a few miles from Knowle Green, found an identity card, a driving licence and an empty wallet on the grass verge. The identity card and driving licence bore the name of George Heath, and the driving licence established that its owner was registered as a public service vehicle driver.

Police to whom the workman handed his finds checked them out, and discovered that a private hire car driver named George Heath had not returned home the previous night and had been reported missing, since this was not in keeping with his regular habits. They also ascertained that the car he had been driving was a Ford V8. On circulating these facts to other police stations in the area, it was soon established that the description of George Heath tallied with the body that had been found at Knowle Green. Formal identification was quickly available.

When police interviewed the night watchman at a factory near the place where Heath's documents had been found, they made a breakthrough. The watchman told them that at around 2.30 a.m. on Saturday, 7 October, he had heard a noise which sounded like a muffled gunshot being fired in a confined space.

Another police breakthrough soon ensued. On Monday, 9 October, a police constable patrolling Lurgan Avenue, off Fulham Palace Road, saw a Ford V8 saloon car parked outside a house. The registration number was one that all police had been alerted to look out for – RD 8955. The constable, named Walters, reported to his station by radio. Detective Inspector Read and other officers arrived in response to the constable's report, having been detailed to keep a close surveillance on the car and the house outside which it was parked.

Their day-long surveillance was rewarded. At 9 p.m. that night a young man was seen to emerge from the house and get into the driving seat of the car. He was wearing a jacket bearing the one gold bar denoting a Second Lieutenant of the US Army. Constable Walters went up to him and said, 'Is this your car, sir?' The young man made no reply. The constable thereupon called to Detective Inspector Read and Sergeant Dowell, who were nearby. The two officers searched the young man and found a Remington automatic pistol in his hip pocket and six rounds of live ammunition in another pocket. He was arrested and taken to Hammersmith Police Station.

On being questioned, the young man said that his name was Richard John Allen and that he was a Second Lieutenant in the 501st Parachute Infantry of the US Army. The police notified the US Army authorities. Meanwhile, they lost no time in arranging for a forensic examination of the car.

A close examination of the car revealed dents in the door and the glove compartment consistent with having been caused by a ricochet from a bullet. The tyre treads were found to match exactly those found on the grass verge beside the ditch in which Heath's body was found.

Forensic scientists next turned their attention to Allen's pistol, which was found to contain six live rounds, one of them in the breech. Both the hammer and the safety catch were off, signifying that the gun was ready to be fired instantly.

The suspect was detained overnight at Hammersmith Police Station, and the following morning he was interviewed by Lieutenant de Mott of the US Army's 8th Military Police (Criminal Investigation Division). Under close interrogation Allen revealed that his real name was Karl Gustav Hulten, a private in the 501st Infantry Parachute Regiment. He admitted that he had been AWOL for about six weeks, and said that the gun found in his possession was his army issue. He said that he always carried it, but maintained that it had never been fired.

He said that he had 'found the car abandoned' in a wood near his base on the afternoon of the day preceding his arrest. It had run out of petrol and oil and one of the tyres was flat. He said that he fetched petrol and oil, and pumped up the tyre, after which he drove it to the house of a girlfriend. The following night, he continued, he was arrested as he left this same house and got into the car which had been parked outside.

Hulten was then asked to account for his movements on the night of the murder. He stated that he had 'slept rough', spending part of the night in an abandoned truck near Newbury, but it was too cramped to be comfortable, so he left at about 5 a.m. and hitch-hiked to London, where he spent the night with a girlfriend. Hulten was then taken to the US Army CID Headquarters in Piccadilly for further questioning. Here he changed his story, saying that he had found the car 'abandoned in a car park' and had driven it off and spent the night with yet another girlfriend. He said that her name was Georgina Grayson, and he offered to take Lieutenant de Mott to her flat and also to show him where he had picked up the car.

On the way to the girl's flat at 311 King Street, Hammersmith, Lieutenant de Mott collected two police inspectors, and the four continued on to the address, where they found the girl in bed. The girl was Betty Jones – who used the stage name of Georgina Grayson. One of the inspectors asked her whether she knew an American soldier named Ricky Allen, alias Karl Gustav Hulten. She replied that she did. She was then questioned as to the dates on which Hulten had stayed at her flat.

'Let me see, now,' she replied. 'I met him on Tuesday. He has stayed here every night since Saturday.'

While Betty was being questioned, Hulten was being subjected to yet another police interrogation, and made yet another statement, which read in part as follows:

> I went to the cinema with a girl. After leaving her, I went to Georgina's house and I suggested that we go for a walk. She went back upstairs to fetch her coat. We had some tea, sandwiches and cakes at a little tea-room which is open all night. We left there at one o'clock in the morning and went back to her flat, where I stayed the night.
>
> The following night we went to the dog racing with Len Bexley. That night we stayed in a hotel at Victoria. On Sunday night we went back to Georgina's flat. On the Monday I abandoned the army truck I had been using and stole a Ford car from a parking lot in Hammersmith. This is the car I was in when I was arrested.
>
> I do not know George Heath and have never met him. I did not know who owned the car I took.

That same afternoon, the police investigation took a dramatic new turn. Henry Kimberley, a War Reserve police constable who had known Betty Jones for several years, had met her in the street. 'You look worried,' he told her. 'What's the problem?'

'It's the coppers,' she replied. 'You've read about this Heath murder case? They've been questioning me about it.'

'Why?' her companion queried. 'After all, you didn't bump him off, did you?'

'No, but I know the man they have as a suspect – in fact he is my boyfriend. But he could not have done it, because he spent all Friday night with me.' Then, suddenly, after a short pause, she continued, almost as an afterthought: 'If you'd seen someone do what I've seen done, you wouldn't be able to sleep all night either.'

Later that day, Kimberley brooded upon this last remark. What did Betty mean? It sounded very suspicious to him. Eventually he decided that it would be in everyone's best interests to report the suspicious conversation to the police, who sent him with an inspector in a car to bring Betty in for questioning. On the way to the police station, Betty decided to unburden herself of this intolerable knowledge. Quite suddenly, with no prompting, she burst out. 'I was in the car when Heath was shot. I didn't do it.'

At the police station she was cautioned, and then admitted to having been involved in a number of crimes with Hulten since 3 October when she had met him. On the Friday afternoon Hulten had left her flat at about 4.30, saying that he would be back at about six o'clock, but he did not turn up until 11.30. 'Let's go out and do a job,' he said. They went out and walked along Hammersmith Road, and stood together in a shop doorway opposite Cadby Hall. After about ten minutes or so, a dark-coloured Ford car approached them, very slowly, like a cab looking for business. Hulten hailed it, and Betty went over to the kerb to speak to the driver.

Betty's statement ran:

I asked him whether he was a cab, and he replied, 'Private hire. Where do you want to go?' I told the driver to wait while I asked Ricky, who asked me how many people were there in the car, and I told him, 'Only the driver.' We both went across to the car and Ricky told the driver to take us to the top of King Street. I now know that the driver's name was George Heath. He told Ricky that the fare would be ten shillings, and Ricky said, 'That's OK.' Ricky and I sat in the rear seat. After a little while the driver said, 'We are now in the Great West Road.' Ricky then told the driver to drive slowly so that we could look out for the place we wanted to get to. After about another 300 yards, we came to a bridge. 'This will do,' Ricky said, 'we'll get out here.'

I heard a click and saw that Ricky was holding his automatic in his right hand. I realized that he intended to frighten the driver into giving him his money. The driver stopped the car and leaned across the back of his seat with the obvious intention of opening the nearside door for me to get out. Ricky was sitting on my right. Just as the driver leaned over to open the door, I saw a flash and heard a bang. Then I heard Ricky say to the driver, 'Move over or I'll give you another lot.' I could see that the driver was too badly wounded to move. Ricky then got out and went round to the driver's door, got into the car and pushed the man out of his way, slid behind the wheel and drove off at speed. He seemed to drive a long way.

By this time Heath was beyond all help. The bullet had hit his spine, paralysing him. His breathing came in short laboured gasps, but after about fifteen minutes it stopped. Ricky then – according to the next part of Betty's statement – told her to pull down a rear window-blind and check whether they were being followed by another car. No one was in sight at that hour. Ricky continued driving until London had been left behind and they were well into the country.

Betty went on:

While he was driving along, he told me to look for the driver's wallet in the inside breast pocket of his jacket. There was no wallet there, so I looked in his other pockets. I found the wallet in the left-hand pocket of his overcoat. It contained four pounds. I put the wallet on the rear seat. I also found his identity card, a cheque book, a driving licence, some petrol coupons and some assorted papers, letters and snapshots. In his trouser pockets I found a pound in silver coins and a few pennies, which I put into my pocket. I also found a brown leather-covered cigarette-case. There was also a matching lighter. I put these, too, into my pocket. Ricky asked me if he was wearing a watch. There was one on his left wrist. I took it off and handed it to Ricky. He then told me to look on the floor of the car to see if I could find the bullet. He gave me a torch to do this. I could not find any bullet.

According to Betty's statement, Ricky then drove on until, by taking a turning off the main road, he reached a common. He drove on to the grass and stopped two or three yards from a ditch. He got out of the car, dragged the body from the car and rolled it into the ditch. He told Betty that he had blood on his hands, and Betty gave him one of Heath's handkerchiefs, taken from his pockets, to wipe his hands. He then made a U-turn and drove back to the main road.

On the return journey, the girl made a further search with the torch for the bullet, and this time she found it, on the floor by the nearside door. Ricky then told Betty to take over the driving because he wanted to look through the various items that she had taken from the dead man's pockets. While she was driving, Ricky opened one of the windows and threw some of the items from it. He also jettisoned the bullet in the same manner, aiming for a clump of bushes. The bullet was never found. After removing the money from the wallet, he threw this out of the window.

Betty's statement then continued:

> Just before we reached the roundabout near which Ricky had shot the driver, I asked him if he knew the name of the place where he had dumped the body, and he said it was Staines. After reaching this roundabout, Ricky took the wheel again, and drove the car eventually into the old Gaumont Cinema car park behind Hammersmith Broadway. We left the car and walked along the Broadway until we reached the Black and White Café, which was open all night. It was a quarter to four by their clock when we had something to eat. There were quite a lot of cab drivers there, and I asked Ricky to see whether one of them would drive us home. None of them would.

Betty then volunteered the information that before leaving the car they wiped it inside and out with their handkerchiefs to remove any fingerprints. They must have made a good job of it, because the forensic experts who examined the car stated that the only fingerprints found in or on the car were those of the dead man and a

few others, not the suspect couple's, but probably those of
previous fare-paying passengers.

Betty went on:

> After leaving the car, we walked home. When we got in, I
> said to Ricky, 'He's dead, isn't he?' He said, 'Yes.' 'How
> could you do it – a cold-blooded murder like that?' I asked
> him. He told me, 'People in my profession haven't the time
> to think what they do.' 'What do mean – your profession?'
> I asked him. 'Do you mean a professional robber?' No,'
> Ricky answered, 'I'm a professional soldier.' We then
> examined the things we had taken from the dead man, and
> then went to bed. The next day we rose at about eleven
> o'clock. Ricky went out and came back at a quarter to
> three. He told me that he had sold the watch to the barber
> who had a shop next door to the all-night café on
> Hammersmith Broadway where we had had our meal. He
> told me to get ready for an outing to the dog track.

On the Sunday night they went to the car park where
they had left the Ford V8 car. 'It's still here,' Ricky told his
companion. 'There's nothing to worry about. There's
nothing in the newspapers, and the police haven't found
the body yet.' They took the car that same night and went
to Reading. Later Betty was to tell police that the only time
Ricky had given her any money was when they had been
to the dogs, when he gave her money to bet with. She won
£7.00.

Hulton was still being questioned intensively. He
admitted having shot Heath, but claimed that it had been
accidental. He said he had drawn the gun merely to
frighten Heath, but had failed to leave the safety catch on,
and it had gone off unintentionally while he was
distracted by the girl's talking.

*   *   *

The trial opened in January 1945 when Betty Jones was
just marginally over eighteen years of age, which meant
that she was on trial for her life, for if she had been a few
days younger she would have been too young to receive
the death sentence. The trial made legal history by being

the first time a serving American soldier had appeared before a British court on a capital charge.

Karl Gustav Hulten's defence of the shooting having been accidental was easily refuted by the prosecution, and his own fate appeared inevitable. But the public, doubtless at least partly influenced by the girl's youth and exceptional beauty, wondered whether her defence – that she had been unduly influenced, coerced or even afraid of her companion in crime, rang true. The prosecution made much of the fact that all the numerous witnesses they produced who had seen Betty in Hulten's company were agreed that on none of these occasions had the female defendant shown any apparent fear of him, or seemed to be under his coercion. Under British law, she was equally culpable with the man who had fired the fatal shot. She was found guilty, and sentence of death was duly passed upon her, despite the plea of recommendation to mercy entered by the jury on account of her youth. She was led to the cells below the courtroom, screaming at her conspirator in crime, 'It's lies, all lies! Why don't you tell the truth?'

Just forty-eight hours before she would have met the hangman, Betty Jones was reprieved, her sentence being commuted to life imprisonment. With remission for good behaviour, she served only nine years. Asked by a newspaper reporter what she felt when she knew that Hulten had been hanged, she replied, 'It's perhaps just as well that he's dead. I wouldn't have wanted to see him again.'

3

The Black Widow

Lyda Ambrose (1921)

Edward Myer was a 6 ft 4 in, strapping specimen of a man, but for all that he was shy and retiring in disposition. He was not one to be seen patronizing the town taverns in the town of Twin Falls, Idaho, or attending the weekly dances to look over the available female talent. So it caused quite a stir when one day he returned home to the farm where he was employed as head stockman from a weekend in Twin Falls, bringing with him a bride.

The woman Ed has chosen for his helpmeet was no blushing virgin. In fact Lyda was not only eleven years her husband's senior, but she had been married before to a man named William McHaffie, a café owner in Twin Falls. Unfortunately the marriage had not lasted, but it was not a question of incompatibility or divorce: McHaffie had died suddenly quite soon after the knot had been tied.

While the gossips wondered aloud why Ed had chosen a widow so much older than himself, everyone liked Lyda. She was good-looking, soft-spoken, and always ready to lend a hand when a neighbour had work to be done that needed a woman's touch. Bud Taylor, the owner of Blue Lakes Farm, was glad that his head stockman had found such an attractive wife and settled down; he was by far the best stockman for miles, and it was hardly likely that he would want to leave now that he had married. Bud increased his wages, and Ed threw himself into his work with his usual enthusiasm and devotion to the animals entrusted to his care.

Six weeks after Ed had returned home with his bride, he

was suddenly taken sick. He woke in the middle of the night with violent pains in his stomach, then he vomited. Trembling and sweating, he threw off the bedclothes although it was winter, complaining of an unbearable heat. The colour of his face was ghastly. Lyda knew that he was in a bad way, and that she had to fetch the doctor fast. She lost no time but threw on her outdoor clothes and ran to the main farmhouse, several hundred yards from their tied cottage, to rouse Bud Taylor.

As Bud was bending over his groaning and writhing foreman, he knew that Ed needed more than just a doctor – he must be taken to hospital at once. He ran back to the farmhouse and saddled the pony and somehow got it between the shafts of the sulky (a two-wheeled pony-trap). Together he and Lyda got the sick man into the vehicle, and at 4 a.m. Ed was admitted to the Twin Falls General Hospital. He was attended by Dr Edwin Graham and Dr Ronald Kimball. But despite everything that their combined efforts could do for him, Ed Myer died at 2 p.m. on the same day, 20 November 1920, as Bud Taylor and Lyda waited at the bedside. For the second time in three years Lyda had become a widow, and Bud Taylor was without a foreman for his farm.

Bud Taylor was good to Lyda. He saw her through the funeral, and helped her straighten out her financial affairs. When Lyda told Bud that Ed had carried no life insurance, Bud told her that she could stay on at the farm for as long as she liked. Lyda looked at him through tear-misted eyes. 'You've been so good to me,' she said with a wan smile. 'I don't know what I would have done without you. But I can't stay on. I have to get a job. So I will be returning to Twin Falls.'

Taylor nodded sympathetically, and later that week drove Lyda and her suitcases into the town, not without regret. Then he set about looking for a new stockman to replace his late foreman, who had been well liked and was missed by all at the farm. And most probably he would not have questioned the mysterious illness that had brought about Ed's death in so short a time, if it had not been for a call he received from the manager of the Cattlemen's

Mutual Life Insurance Company in Twin Falls, who wished to speak to Lyda. Taylor informed him that she had left for Twin Falls, but he did not know her address. 'Is it important?' Bud asked.

'Not if you don't think 12,000 dollars important,' was the reply.

'What 12,000 dollars?' asked the mystified Taylor.

'That's the amount of the policy Mr Myer was carrying,' the manager replied. 'Mrs Myer is the beneficiary. I have some papers for her to sign.'

'But I thought she told me ...' began Taylor, then stopped abruptly.

'What were you going to say?'

'Oh, nothing in particular. If I hear from her, I'll tell her to get in touch with you, OK?'

All that day Bud was thoughtful. He was certain that Lyda had told him that Ed carried no insurance ... and how come that Ed, who had never had a day's illness in his life, had died so suddenly? Twelve thousand dollars! That was a lot of insurance. Why had Lyda lied?

After a sleepless night, Bud saddled up the next morning and drove into town to see the sheriff, E.R. Sherman, and his deputy, Virgil Ormsby. He told them of Myer's sudden marriage and his even more sudden death only six weeks later. He told them of his discussion with Lyda after the funeral, and the call from the insurance company manager. 'Why would Lyda have lied about the insurance,' he said, 'unless she was trying to cover up something? Like, say, a motive for killing Ed?'

The sheriff leaned back in his chair, puffing at his pipe. 'Now take it easy, Bud!' he cautioned. 'I know how you feel about Myer. But don't go off at half-cock. Jumping to hasty conclusions will get us nowhere. About that insurance – lots of folks don't like to discuss their private financial arrangements with strangers. That's reasonable, isn't it?'

'Yes, come to think of it, I suppose it is,' Bud agreed.

'I've known Lyda for years,' the sheriff continued. 'Never heard a bad word about her. She has a good reputation here in town.'

Taylor fidgeted uneasily in his chair. He was obviously

not convinced. 'Didn't her first husband die about three years ago – Bill McHaffie, who ran the Griddle Café?'

'Yes, he did,' Sherman replied, 'but there's no law to say a widow can't remarry.'

'You're right, of course,' Bud had to agree. 'But when her second husband dies – and mighty suddenly at that ... why, the honeymoon was hardly over!'

'I see what you're driving at,' the sheriff conceded. 'How do you think Myer died?'

'Poison!' replied Bud emphatically. 'I got to thinking about it last night, after that insurance man called.'

'Did he and Lyda eat with you?'

'No. They cooked for themselves in their foreman's cottage.'

The sheriff was thoughtful for a moment. Then he spoke. 'OK, Bud. We'll probe around a bit and see what we come up with. But don't bank on our coming up with *anything*. And keep your suspicions to yourself. Not a word to anybody.'

When Taylor had gone, the sheriff turned to his deputy. 'Well, what do you think?'

Ormsby rolled a cigarette and shook his head. 'Too bad about Myer kicking the bucket,' he observed, 'but I can't imagine Lyda having anything to do with it. Why, when she waited table for Bill McHaffie before she married him, she served me my ham and eggs many a time. A nicer woman I never met.'

'Well, you know the old saying – you can't judge a book by its cover. An exhumation of Myer's body would tell if he was poisoned or not, but we have no proof. We can't get an order for an exhumation without at least solid grounds for suspicion. Just think how foolish we'd look if he was found to have died from natural causes! No, we'll have to let it ride. We don't want to raise any dust. We can just keep an ear out for any rumours.'

Ormsby pushed back his chair. 'I think we ought to make a few very discreet inquiries,' he said. 'Wouldn't do any harm.'

'Well, you could start with the hospital,' Sherman agreed.

Shortly afterwards, Deputy Sheriff Virgil Ormsby was

deep in conversation with Dr Kimball at Twin Falls General Hospital. He recalled the case very well, since at the time there had been a slight disagreement between himself and Dr Graham over the diagnosis of the case. 'I contended that it was typhoid,' he said, 'while my colleague said that he thought it was ptomaine poisoning. The autopsy showed that I was right – there were traces of typhoid germs in the body.'

'Who obtained the order for the autopsy?'

'Why, if I remember rightly, Mrs Myer was very anxious for it to be carried out,' the doctor said.

Ormsby rolled another cigarette. 'Tell me, Doc,' he said, 'just what were Myer's symptoms?'

'Violent stomach cramps and convulsions.'

'Could those symptoms be consistent with poisoning?'

Dr Kimball looked up sharply. 'Yes, they could, but ...'

'When you carried out the autopsy,' Ormsby persisted, 'you didn't think of looking for poison, did you?'

'No, we did not. There were no grounds for suspicion as to the cause of death ...' He broke off abruptly. 'Are you trying to suggest that Myer was *murdered*?'

'I'm not trying to suggest anything, Doc,' Ormsby said. 'It's just a routine check. I'd be obliged if you don't mention my talk with you to anyone.'

Ormsby's next call was at the offices of the Cattlemen's Mutual Life Insurance Company, where the 'routine check' took on more serious overtones. The previous day Lyda Myer had come into the office, signed the necessary papers and picked up a cheque for 12,000 dollars.

'Tell me,' Ormsby said, 'when did Mr Myer take out that policy?'

The office manager went to a filing cabinet and looked into a file. 'Just six weeks ago,' he said. 'He took it out on 6 October.' Ormsby's thoughts could be more easily conjectured than described. It was about six weeks ago that Myer and Lyda had been married.

'Tell me,' Ormsby continued, 'did Mr Myer take a physical examination for this policy?'

'Of course,' was the reply. 'For a policy of that amount we insist on it.'

'And how did he shape up?'

'According to the doctor's report he was in perfect health. Say – what's this all about?'

'Oh, just a few routine questions,' Ormsby replied.

His next port of call was the bank on which the cheque had been drawn. The manager informed him that on the previous day Lyda Myer had cashed her insurance cheque, taking the proceeds in large-denomination bills, which she stuffed loose into her handbag. Even the bank manager had thought it rather strange that she should take the 12,000 dollars in cash, and suggested that she open an account with the money, but she had said she was intending to purchase a restaurant and needed the money in cash. He also volunteered the information that, although Lyda did not bank with them, they did know her, and had heard about her husband's untimely death. They had known him, too. The bank manager was also able to inform the deputy sheriff of Lyda's address – a hotel in the town.

On arriving post-haste at the hotel, Ormsby was not unduly surprised to discover that Lyda had checked out the day before, leaving no forwarding address.

When Ormsby reported back to his superior, Sherman had news for him. While his deputy had been gathering information from the various calls he had made, the sheriff had been checking on Lyda's previous husband, William McHaffie. He found that they had been married on 10 June 1918, and that two weeks later he had sold the Griddle Café in Twin Falls and bought a small ranch in Hardin, Montana. Four months after the couple had moved to the ranch, McHaffie was suddenly taken ill and died on 22 October.

'Any insurance?' Ormsby queried.

'No, but Lyda got the ranch,' Sherman said.

'What did McHaffie die from?'

'Stomach ulcer, according to the death certificate.'

Ormsby snorted in disbelief. 'Stomach ulcer my eye!' he exploded. 'Bill McHaffie was as hale and hearty a man as Ed Myer – probably more so as he was younger. What do we do now?'

'Before she married McHaffie, Lyda's name was Dooley. She came from Keytesville, Missouri. Go there and see what you can find out about her.'

'She's skipped town – what do I do if I find her there? Do I bring her in?'

'Hey, not so fast! No. Keep out of her way. We can't move yet until we have something definite to go on. Just keep her under observation, if she is there, and report to me. After all, it's not a crime for a woman to be twice widowed. This whole thing might blow up in our faces.'

Ormsby left for Missouri the same evening, arriving in Keytesville the following morning. Checking in at the local police headquarters, he was not unduly surprised to learn that Lyda Dooley was well known in the town, but more surprised to learn that Dooley was not her maiden name. According to the police, Lyda's maiden name was Ambrose, and in 1917, at the age of twenty-six, she had married Robert Dooley, the son of a prosperous local farmer.

'And what happened to Bob?' asked Ormsby.

The police officer shrugged expressively. 'Now that's a family which had mighty rough luck. Bob was a nice young fellow. He and Lyda had hardly ended their honeymoon when Bob took sick and died. Old man Dooley was a broken man, losing two sons one after another.'

'*Two* sons?'

'Yes. Bob's brother Ed. Younger brother of Bob. He died about three months before.'

'What did Ed die from?'

'Stomach trouble. Same as Bob.'

Ormsby drove out to the Dooley farm, where he found the father of the two boys who had died, mending a harness in the barn. Though well into his sixties and standing over six feet tall, old Dooley was still strong and vigorous. No stomach trouble there, Ormsby mused to himself as he walked up to the farmer.

'I'm looking for Lyda,' he said. 'Has she been to see you at all lately?'

Dooley dropped his tools and stared hard at the deputy

sheriff. 'No, she hasn't,' he said, 'and she'd better not show her face hereabouts.'

'Why not?'

'She murdered my two boys, that's why!'

'Have you proof?' Ormsby's heart began to beat fast.

'Proof? If I had proof, I'd have had the law on her a long time ago!' The old farmer spat in disgust. 'But I *know* she murdered 'em.'

'Why?'

'For their insurance, that's why!'

'But she was only married to Bob, not Ed.'

'Sure, she was only married to Bob. But that never stopped her. Ed was sweet on her and was all set to marry her, when he took sick and died. He already had a policy in her favour. After Ed's death Bob took up with her, and he took out insurance, too. They each took out 2,500 dollars. Two finer boys you never saw. Big, strapping fellows, as strong as an ox. Never had a day sick in their lives. Never even caught measles or chicken-pox as babies. Nor the mumps nor the whooping-cough neither. Then they started horsing around with that woman, and both were dead in three months.'

The old man went on to tell Ormsby how Lyda had played off one brother against the other, and then, when she had collected the insurance on both of them, she cleared out. 'I was hoping you law fellers would catch up with her one day. Who's she murdered now?'

'We don't know,' replied Ormsby cautiously. 'We're just checking. What were the symptoms when your boys died?'

'Stummick. Terrible pains in the stummick. Them fool doctors – what do they know? Ulcers, they said. Said it must be the water here on the farm. Rubbish! Look at me – I've been drinking the water from that well for over sixty years, and I haven't got any ulcers. My boys never had any either – do you think I wouldn't have known? They were poisoned by that woman!'

The following day Ormsby was back in Twin Falls and reporting his conversation with the farmer to Sherman, who by now was convinced that the time had come for action. The death of two husbands, he said, could be pure coinicidence, but three husbands and a brother-in-law, all dying from violent stomach symptoms and all within a few months, or even weeks, of being ministered to by Lyda, was stretching coincidence too far. The whole thing smacked of murder.

A conference was held with DA Frank Stephens and Chief of Police Robert Armstead. A court order was obtained and Ed Myer's body quietly disinterred. The autopsy was performed by the state chemist, Edward Rodenbaugh and the county coroner, P.T. Grossmann. Three hours later they were able to report that Myer's body contained enough arsenic to kill a dozen men. Traces of typhoid were also found, as previously reported, but these could have been picked up from impure drinking water anywhere on the ranchlands territory and were not in sufficient quantity to have caused death.

Three more bodies were exhumed, and autopsies performed. The reports on all three of them were identical. William McHaffie, Robert Dooley and his brother Edward had died from arsenical poisoning.

'My God,' Sherman exclaimed after he had read the four autopsy reports, 'that woman puts Bluebeard to shame. We must nab her quick, before she marries some other poor devil.'

The DA put in a cautionary note. 'Just taking her in is not enough,' he warned. 'We will have to prove that she had access to the poison. He turned to the police chief. 'That's your department, Bob. Check every drugstore – cover the whole state if you have to. See if you can find someone who sold that woman arsenic.'

While this was going on, another search was also being conducted for the much-married and oft-widowed Lyda Ambrose-Dooley-McHaffie-Myer. Would she strike again? But the elusive black widow, like the spider with its deadly venom, was nowhere to be found. She had dropped out of sight after cashing her 12,000-dollar cheque as completely as if she had vanished from the face of the earth. Which the searchers were sure she had not done, knowing her propensity for seeking out another willing dupe to be lured to his death at the drop of a pen on an insurance policy proposal form.

Three days passed with no breakthrough in the case. Ormsby was possessed by fear that Lyda, wherever she might be, could by this time have already lined up another victim. Ormsby got the approval of his superior to go out to the abandoned ranch in Montana where Lyda had lived with McHaffie. It proved to be a smart move and led to the discovery of yet another murder.

Ormsby naturally wanted to know whether McHaffie had taken out a life policy in Lyda's favour, and on arriving in the Montana town the first thing he did was to make the rounds of all the insurance offices. On his third call he struck oil. Ted Russell, the manager of the firm, had known McHaffie well. He had known Lyda, too.

'That dame's no good,' he told Ormsby. 'Something fishy there. He was going to take out a policy, but he died before he could sign the papers. Next thing you know, she had remarried without batting an eyelid. Met the guy right here in my office – one of my own good friends, Harlan C. Lewis. He fell for that woman like a ton of bricks and McHaffie had not been dead and buried long before they married. I tried to warn him that she was up to no good, but he wouldn't have it. He got me to make him out a 10,000 dollar policy. *She* must have put him up to it. Not two months later, he was dead.'

'What did he die from?'

'Doctor said it was the flu, but I don't believe it. Harlan Lewis was one of my best friends – I'd known him since we were boys in school together. Never even caught a cold in his life. Flu, my grandmother's foot! That woman bumped him off, that's for sure. But I had no proof. What could I do without proof?'

'So why did you feel so sure Lyda had murdered him?' queried Ormsby.

'Stands to reason, doesn't it?' the manager replied. 'Two husbands dead in less than a couple of months. The widow inherits a ranch from the first and 10,000 dollars in insurance from the second. What do you think?'

'I can't think anything without proof,' said Ormsby. He

wondered what Russell would think had he known of the deaths of the two Dooley brothers and Ed Myer ...

'Where did Lewis die? At home or in the hospital?' he asked.

'At the McHaffie ranch.'

'And that's where McHaffie died, too?'

'Yes.'

'Could you drive me out there?' asked Ormsby. 'A private car would not arouse any comment, whereas my police car might, and we have to keep things a bit quiet if we are to try find any evidence that what you think might be true. Can you do this?'

'Sure,' was the reply. 'I'll do anything if it will help you find out the truth. The McHaffie place has stood unoccupied since Harlan died. Lyda moved out right afterwards, but I never heard that she put it up for sale. The funeral was the last place anyone saw her, and no one knows where she went to.'

The ranch was weed-grown, the fencing broken and the whole aspect was of a forlorn and abandoned homestead. But as Russell drove up to the house, Ormsby was quick to spot the impressions of recent tyre tracks in the dust. Someone had been to the house before them.

Another singular feature was the presence of a new and strong lock on the front door of the ranch house. It was not rusty and creaking like other hardware on the premises. In fact, the new lock was so strong that it would not budge, and Ormsby had to force a window and climb into the house, followed by Russell.

Despite the abandoned look of the place from the outside, there was ample evidence that the house had been used very recently. The furniture had been dusted and polished, and there were food dishes in the kitchen sink. Two glasses stood beside an empty wine bottle, and a full ashtray was nearby. Cigar stubs lay among the ashes. Upstairs, in the master bedroom the bed was rumpled and unmade, and twin head impressions were on the pillows. Two persons had slept in that bed. What a turn-up for the book, Ormsby mused. His heart was pounding with excitement. Had it been Lyda, the black widow, with another potential victim? Had she in truth murdered four husbands and a brother-in-law? Was she even now talking her latest conquest into insuring his life for thousands of dollars as a prerequisite to a wedding? If so, would he be too late to stop her in her tracks before a sixth victim was ensnared in her net, unable to escape?

Ormsby turned to his companion. 'It couldn't be trespassers,' he observed. 'If so, the place would have been broken into. Whoever used this place in the last couple of days had a key to the front door. And who would have a key but Lyda? I'd say it was her – with a man. She's a fast worker.'

'What are you going to do?' asked Russell. 'Keep the place under surveillance? Maybe they'll be back.'

Ormsby shook his head. 'I don't think so. From the dishes in the sink and the cigar stubs, they were here for only a couple of days. They've gone.'

'We'll search the place while we're here,' the deputy sheriff said. 'We might find something.' And find something he did – an old envelope which had been used to scribble a recipe on. But it was the name and address on the other side of the envelope that caught Ormsby's attention: Frank Lovett, 22 South Chippewa Street, Twin Falls, Idaho. Ormsby knew that Frank Lovett, besides being the owner of a prosperous garage business, was also one of the most eligible bachelors in town. Was he destined to be Lyda's next victim?

Ormsby pocketed the envelope and turned back to his meticulous search. High on a top shelf in the pantry adjoining the kitchen, he found fourteen packets of flypapers. These were not the sticky, tanglefoot type; they were squares of a black, spongy paper impregnated with arsenic – a variety long since banned by law. When immersed in water, the arsenic is liberated and is deadly to flies – and man. So this was where Lyda had obtained her supplies of arsenic. No wonder that the police had failed to trace a single pharmacist who had sold her arsenic. The deadly flypapers could be bought without question at any corner stores.

Ormsby had the evidence he needed. Taking leave of

Russell, he headed back to Twin Falls. Arriving the next morning, he was informed by Sherman that the search for Lyda was progressing apace and that Frank Lovett was being sought urgently, as a result of the telephone call that Ormsby had put through to the office before leaving Montana. Inquiries at Lovett's garage had revealed that he had left town in his car and that none of his employees knew where he had gone, nor had they heard from him since. A description of his car and its licence number had been put out, as also a description of Lyda, but no trace of the missing couple had come to light.

Ormsby was detailed to contact every insurance office in the state. He was engaged in this boringly repetitive task when, quite unexpectedly, the object of their search walked nonchalantly into the office. Lovett greeted the sheriff, whom he knew, enthusiastically. 'Hi! I heard you want to see me. What's it all about?'

'Where's Lyda?' Sherman said.

Lovett took the cigar from his mouth. 'Lyda?'

'Yes, Lyda. Were you at her ranch house in Hardin, Montana, lately?'

Lovett flushed uncomfortably. 'What if I was? Is that against the law?'

'Were you there, Frank?' the sheriff persisted.

'Yes, I was. But I'll be goddamned if I know how you found out.'

'Did she come back to Twin Falls with you?'

'No.'

'Did you marry her?'

'*Marry* her? Good God, no. I'm not the marrying kind. But she did go on a bit about marriage. I can't blame her for wanting to get herself another husband. A widow can get lonesome. But me? I like my freedom and I intend to keep it.'

'You can thank your lucky stars for that,' Sherman said.

Lovett looked bewildered. 'Why all this interest in Lyda?' he asked. 'OK, so she's been married twice already. She's had a rough deal – they both died in a short while.'

Sherman laughed, but his laugh was without humour. 'Frank,' he said, 'that woman has had four husbands, never mind two. All four of them died in a few weeks. Lyda stuffed them all full of arsenic. You were marked for the fifth.'

The cigar fell from Lovett's lips, and he sank into his chair. 'You gotta be kidding!'

'No kidding,' Sherman rejoined soberly. 'What happened when you told her that marriage was not on the cards?'

'She walked out on me,' Lovett said. 'Said she wasn't interested in one-night stands, only marriage. She asked me to see her off to San Francisco. Probably thought there would be more choice there than in a one-horse Montana town.' Lovett smiled ruefully. 'A pity, though – she was a real classy dame.'

Wires hummed and the police were alerted in San Francisco, and Sherman and his deputy twiddled their thumbs impatiently for three weeks before news came through that they had at last traced the elusive deadly widow in the Bay City. She had married a man named Paul Southard in Oakland, across the bay. He was still alive and kicking, because he was a naval officer and the day after they were married his ship sailed for Honolulu. The very next day his bride sailed to Hawaii to join him. The police were now trying to locate her in Hawaii.

Sherman and Ormsby sweated out the next few hours while a man's life hung in the balance. Then the desperately awaited call at last came through. Paul Southard was safe and well aboard his ship, and Lyda had been located in Honolulu, arrested and put behind bars.

Five indictments for murder were lined up against Lyda, but it was for the slaying of Ed Myer that she went on trial, in September 1921. Although ably defended by a top Twin Falls lawyer, he could not explain away the lethal dose of arsenic found in Myer's body. A verdict of guilty was brought in, and Madame Bluebeard was sentenced to life imprisonment in the state penitentiary.

Ten years later, on 4 May 1931 Lyda made a spectacular escape from prison, with the aid of a former inmate of the adjacent men's prison. First she sawed her way out of her cell, then scaled a thirty-foot wall with the aid of a ladder which had been put conveniently in place for her to use.

Lyda had exactly one year of freedom, during which time it is not known how many men, if any, she married and poisoned before collecting their insurance. When she was picked up in Kansas City in May 1932 she had a man with her at the time; evidently ten years in prison had not dimmed her fatal charms. She was returned to the prison from which she had made her escape, there to serve out the rest of her sentence, until her death.

Frank Lovett no doubt followed her career with interest, at the same time continuing to thank his lucky stars that he was not the marrying kind.

4

The Prophetess of Death

Betty Eccles (1843)

Life had been hard for Harry Eccles. His first wife had died in childbirth at the age of twenty-four, leaving him with two older children to support as well as the new baby. Work was scarce in the Bolton suburb of Turner Bridge at that time, and he was forced to travel eight miles each way every day by bicycle to work in a Manchester mill. A neighbour, Betty Haslem, looked after the children in his home every day while he was at work.

Before long Harry decided that Betty, a 38-year-old widow herself, would make him a good second wife, despite the fact that she was ten years his senior, and accordingly they were married in January 1841. At this time he found it easier to take lodgings in Manchester during the working week and cycle to that city every Sunday evening, returning on the following Saturday evening. Betty looked after the children very well – he had no fault to find with her at all. Her cooking, cleaning and washing were all accomplished with the minimum of fuss and no diminution of care for the children. So Harry was contented, and counted himself a lucky man. The mill was hard work and he did not much enjoy his digs in Manchester or being away from Betty and his family, but there was nothing he could do about it. Unemployment was rife in Turner Bridge.

In June 1842 a ten-month-old baby named William Heywood, whom Betty nursed for a neighbour, suddenly died while in her care. The local doctor was called, and stated that the baby had had a fatal convulsion, or fit. The baby was buried, his parents mourned, and Betty continued as usual. No one blamed Betty for the fact that the death had occurred when she was looking after the baby while his mother worked.

Three months later, on 8 September, Betty's own ten-year-old daughter from her first marriage, Alice Haslem, died suddenly at home. She had been bright and cheerful on the Sunday evening when Harry had left home for Manchester; when he came home on the following Saturday she was dead and already buried. 'She had a fit,' explained Betty through floods of tears.

As Harry comforted his wife, he prayed that this would be the last of the family's misfortunes, but his wife made a most strange remark. 'Troubles always come in threes,' Betty sobbed. 'We shall have another death in this house before long!' And she would not be comforted. Harry was a bit superstitious and had some misgivings, but he told his wife that her imagination was running away with her.

A fortnight later the prophetess of death's prediction came true. Harry's eldest son William, who was a child of his first marriage, died as suddenly as his stepsister had done, on 26 September. Betty convinced Harry that the child had suffered from a stomach inflammation, and Harry seemed to accept this with a resigned feeling that misfortune was his inevitable lot. Yet another funeral took place.

This time neighbours began to talk. Turner Bridge was not a very big community, and tongue-wagging was a favourite occupation of the women – and the men who had no jobs to go to. Soon afterwards, the police came knocking on Harry Eccles's door. Betty's explanation of the cause of her stepson's death did not satisfy them, and police surgeon Mr Joseph Denham was detailed to carry out a post-mortem on the boy's body. An exhumation order was obtained, and the autopsy duly took place.

Mr Denham found that, although the external appearance of the body was normal and it seemed that the boy had been healthy enough, the lining of the stomach and intestinal tract was red and inflamed. Analysis of the stomach contents revealed the presence of between thirty-three and thirty-five grains of arsenic.

It was then decided to exhume the body of Alice Haslem, the stepsister of the dead boy, who had predeceased him by only eighteen days from a supposed fit. The ensuing autopsy confirmed the presence of arsenic in her stomach and intestinal tract also.

It was discovered that the widow Betty Haslem, in previous years, had had two other children, Hannah and Nancy, both of whom had died before she married Harry Eccles. It was decided to exhume the bodies of these children also, as well as that of the baby William Heywood who had died in Betty's care. The cause of death in his case proved too difficult to determine accurately, and in the case of Hannah Haslem the body was in an advanced stage of decomposition and stomach-contents analysis proved impossible to determine with any degree of accuracy, the results being inconclusive. In the case of Nancy Haslem, however, arsenic was found to be present in the stomach.

The police now had enough evidence to proceed with charges, and on 28 September 1842 Betty Eccles was arrested at her home by Inspector James Harris and charged with the murders of her daughters Alice and Nancy Haslem and her stepson William Eccles. Asked whether she had anything to say, she replied sharply, 'I shall leave that to the court.'

The trial opened in April 1843 at Liverpool Assizes. The first witness for the prosecution was Richard, another stepson and brother of the deceased William. He testified that on the day his brother died, he returned home for lunch from a local mill where he worked, those being the days when even ten-year-old children worked in the mills. On arriving home, he found that his brother, who was also a child mill-worker, had already eaten his meal, and – what was even more unusual – all the dishes had already been washed and put away. It was, he said, the first time he could ever remember that this had happened. Normally their stepmother did not wash the dishes until all the family had partaken of lunch.

Richard also testified that William had told him that he

had eaten damson pudding, a dish which neither Richard nor his sister had been offered. On asking his mother why he and his sister had not had their share, she had told him, 'There was not enough to go round.'

The next witness was ten-year-old Mary Eccles, Betty's stepdaughter, who testified that on the Sunday night following Alice Haslem's death she suggested that she, her brother Richard and their mother visit their stepsister's grave. At this, she continued, Mrs Eccles became quite angry. 'No, we shall not,' she had replied. 'I have enough trouble on my mind already, and we shall have another death in this house before long.'

It seemed that the prophetess of doom had well and truly convicted herself out of her own mouth ...

At this suggestion that she was already planning William's death at that time, Betty jumped to her feet from the dock, shouting 'You're a liar!' at her stepdaughter in the witness-box. The judge rebuked her and told her to refrain from such outbursts, telling her that she would have her say at a later stage.

The next witness called by the prosecution was a Mr Moscrop, proprietor of Moscrop's Stores in Turner Bridge. He said that he himself did not recognize Mrs Eccles or know her personally, but his apprentice, Richard Barlow, did. It was then proposed to call this young man.

Richard Barlow testified that he knew Betty Eccles well as she came into the shop regularly for such items as tea, snuff and so on, and that about six weeks before William Eccles's death she asked for a pennyworth of arsenic, saying that she wanted it to kill mice. The apprentice was not allowed to serve poisons without the presence of the proprietor, who was a qualified chemist, so he called Mr Moscrop. He told Mrs Eccles that the law required that she might only purchase such poisons if she had someone with her as a witness, and refused to sell it to her on that occasion. The woman left the shop and returned some two hours or so later with a woman friend. An ounce of arsenic was duly weighed out, labelled 'Arsenic – Poison', and handed over in return for one penny. No poisons book had to be signed.

The next prosecution witness was John Turner, the head bookkeeper at the firm of Eden and Thwaite, who owned the mill where William had worked. He testified that he met Mrs Eccles for the first time on the day after her daughter Alice died. She had come to see him about money from the burial fund, a charity organized by the firm to help poor employees and their dependants with the costs of family burials.

Mr Turner pointed out to Mrs Eccles that, since neither Alice nor her stepfather had ever worked for the firm, they were not entitled to any benefit from the fund. Nevertheless, because the woman seemed so desperate, Turner gave her ten shillings, which he told her he would dock from her stepson's wages in instalments. He also told her that should any of her stepsons die the family would immediately become entitled to a payment of fifty shillings (£2.50). Not long after this, Turner continued, William Eccles was dead, and Mrs Eccles was back in his office to make a claim for the fifty shillings benefit.

Turner stated that he immediately became suspicious, and delayed making the payment by asking Mrs Eccles to return the following day 'to allow him time for all the paperwork involved'. She did not return the next day, of course, because by then she had been arrested.

Next came the forensic evidence. The dose William had received, stated Dr Watson, the pathologist, was large enough to begin acting within an hour, to fatal effect. Thirty-three to thirty-five grains, he pointed out, was a huge dose – sufficient to kill several men. It was known that William had eaten his lunch at two o'clock and that he had begun vomiting by three. In the meantime, of course, he had returned to the mill for the afternoon's work.

Thomas Davenport, a fellow-worker at the mill, who had helped William home, recalled unexpectedly meeting Mrs Eccles along the way. 'Lad's ill – best give him a cup o' tea,' the man had told her. 'I've got some waiting for him in t'pot,' she replied. But, the prosecution argued, how could she? How could she have known that the boy would be ill? The conclusion to be drawn from this was obvious, counsel stressed.

Mrs Eccles was now called to give evidence on her own behalf. Asked why she had not called a doctor, she stated that she had gone to fetch a Dr Mallet, who lived a few doors away, but the doctor was away. She returned home and gave the boy a cup of tea and some Epsom salts, but he died in agony an hour later.

The defence strove valiantly to prove that the accused had not purchased any poison. They stressed the fact that the woman friend alleged to have accompanied her when she bought the arsenic could not be traced. 'And why not?' counsel said. 'Because she does not exist – there was no purchase of arsenic. Even Mr Moscrop does not remember her.'

'If Mrs Eccles had intended to poison her stepson,' counsel for the defence continued relentlessly, 'would she have gone to a local chemist, where she was known, when she could just as easily have gone to one in Bolton where no one knew her? It stands to reason. As to the motive for the supposed murder, it was said to be the fifty shillings benefit she would have been entitled to from the burial fund. But she would have forfeited all his future earnings of three shillings a week.'

The jury was out for an hour and forty-five minutes, returning a verdict of guilty. Betty remained calm as the death sentence was passed. Asked if she had anything to say, she replied, 'Mercy! My Lord and gentlemen, have mercy upon me!'

But there was to be no mercy for this woman who callously murdered her own children and stepchildren – three certainly, and most probably five. It is interesting to note that Nancy Haslem died in December 1840, just weeks before Betty's marriage to her second husband in January 1841. And records show that both Nancy and Hannah, if they died while her first husband (the girls' father) was employed at one of the local mills, would have entitled the family to receive burial benefits from the funds for the purpose which most mills ran for their employees and their families. These benefits were, of course, usually paid to the mother of the family.

Speculation can go to some lengths, not always

justified, but in this case perhaps one can quote the old saw, that where there's smoke there's fire. What were the circumstances of Betty's first husband's death? Did he die suddenly? He was certainly young – in his late twenties ...

Betty Eccles was executed publicly outside Kirkdale Prison, in Bolton, at twelve o'clock on Saturday, 6 May 1843. As a poisoner, she may not have had the subtlety of a Waddington or a Toppan, but for sheer callousness alone she must surely rank with the worst of wicked women.

5

Thrift in the Kitchen

Anna Zimmermann (1984)

Herr Wilhelm Gruber was not a little annoyed. His employee Josef Wirtz, normally a reliable timekeeper and a man who would have let him know if he could not come in to work owing to illness – had not turned up again. That now made it three days that the 34-year-old barber had not put in an appearance in Herr Gruber's smart gentlemen's hairdressers.

The salon was situated in München gladbach, a thriving town of some 270,000 inhabitants in the great industrial district of the Ruhr in West Germany, not far from the Dutch border. Herr Gruber was puzzled, but he did not have the time to brood over his employee's absence. No doubt there was some plausible explanation for it; perhaps he was too ill to send a message. He knew Wirtz was a loner with few friends and no relatives living nearer than Frankfurt. Gruber shrugged, muttered that no doubt the fellow would turn up in a day or two with some excuse, and got back to the business of cutting hair.

A few streets away from the hairdressing establishment, Josef Wirtz's landlord was taking a more pessimistic view. His tenant had been due to pay his month's rent on his studio apartment on Friday, 1 June 1984, but had not even come home, never mind knocked on his door as he normally did to pay the rent due on the first of each month. The landlord, one Herr Franz-Josef Kreutzer, kept a lookout on Saturday, Sunday and Monday, but still there was no sign of Josef Wirtz. So Kreutzer took his passkey and opened the door to his tenant's apartment, fully expecting to find it stripped of all his personal belongings, signifying that Wirtz had done what is popularly known as a moonlight flit. He was more than a little surprised, therefore, to find that all Wirtz's things were there, even to his toothbrush and shaving gear on the shelf in the bathroom, and a well-stocked refrigerator in the kitchenette. If Wirtz had been intending to do a runner he would have taken at least his personal toiletries and a change of shirts and underwear. Somewhat reassured that the unexplained absence of his tenant was nothing to worry about and that he would turn up soon with the rent and an excuse about being late in paying it, Kreutzer made his way moodily downstairs.

When Monday had passed and Tuesday arrived, and then Wednesday, with no sign of the missing barber, Kreutzer decided to call the police. It was not that he was concerned about his tenant who was, after all, a big strapping six-footer easily able to take care of himself, but the fact that if he had taken it into his head to disappear, then he, the landlord, wished to be able to re-let the studio apartment. His tenants were his living – he did not let the several floors in the old house just for fun. But he could not re-let the flatlet until the previous tenant's possessions had been removed, and to do this he would have to pack them into cartons under police supervision and the police would then seal them and mark them with the police official stamp. Only then could the cartons be stored in the basement of the premises and Kreutzer be free to re-let the apartment. Such was the system – the landlord and the police also keeping an inventory of the stored items, to cover them in the eventuality of the erstwhile tenant's returning; the tenant could not claim that any valuables were missing. If he never came back, the landlord was authorized to appropriate or sell the items after one year.

With Wirtz reported officially missing by his landlord, the police took the personal papers he had left behind and opened an official missing-person file at headquarters, and soon afterwards an officer was detailed to call upon Herr Gruber at his salon and take a statement.

The hairdresser was at a loss to explain the continuing absence of his employee; he had no more idea than the landlord had as to why Wirtz should absent himself without a word of explanation. He described his employee as a reliable and good worker, not given to taking time off, and certainly not without giving prior warning and an acceptable reason. Asked for a description, he said that Wirtz was tall and well built – at least six feet – and had a thick crop of luxuriant wavy black hair, worn shoulder-length, of which he was inordinately proud. He was also handsome, and had a thick black moustache. Herr Gruber added that he thought that Wirtz was rather vain about his appearance – an opinion which was borne out by the police officers who had discovered several studio portraits of the missing barber at his flat.

A description and one of the photographs were circulated throughout West Germany by the police, but no response was forthcoming, and the investigation petered out for lack of clues. Days passed into weeks; Herr Gruber employed a new barber, Herr Kreutzer installed a new tenant in the empty flat, and the police were too busy investigating various crimes to bother about a missing hairdresser. Maybe he had gone missing because he had wanted to; after all, he could always buy a new toothbrush, shaving gear and socks with the money he had omitted to pay in rent. The answer to a policeman's remark, 'Anything new on Wirtz?' was always the same: a non-committal shrug.

* * *

On Saturday, 7 July 1984, a young girl was taking a walk in the Buntergarten, a park at the northern end of Münchengladbach. The park was at its best, with the well-tended lawns and flowerbeds a riot of colour. The girl left the footpath – ignoring the 'keep off the grass' signs – and went to look more closely at one of the circular flowerbeds and sniff the perfume of the stocks, sweetwilliams and other floral delights which surrounded the more inaccessible roses in the middle. As she did so

she became aware that, not entirely masked by the
perfume wafting from the flowerbed, a smell of a
distinctly unpleasant nature was emanating from a small
clump of ornamental shrubs and small trees which
adjoined the flowerbed behind the lawn area. She decided
to investigate; perhaps a dead cat lay there, and she could
ask one of the park-keepers to bury it.

The odour increased in intensity as she moved nearer,
and as she entered the thickest part of the shrubbery she
saw, to her horror, what looked like a human skull, with
dark hair and rotting flesh still adhering to it. It seemed to
have rolled out from an open black plastic dustbin bag
which was lying nearby. There were other bags lying
about, too, in the immediate vicinity, tied up with string.
The girl let out a shriek and fled from the scene, valiantly
stifling a desire to be sick, and rushed to find the nearest
park-keeper.

Detectives were soon at the scene and the park was
sealed off. Anyone attempting to enter or leave was
stopped and their identification checked. At the time, it
could not be determined whether the skull and the bags
had been recently left there, or whether they had been
there for some time. Only a pathologist would be able to
ascertain that.

An examination was arranged, after the remains had
been photographed *in situ*, and the police pathologist was
able to determine that the skull and other remains had
been exposed to the elements for at least forty-eight hours,
this being based on the stage of maggot activity. The
doctor considered, however, that death had occurred
some considerable time earlier – perhaps several weeks,
and that it had not taken place at the spot where the
remains had been discovered. They had merely been
transported there in the plastic bags for disposal, probably
in the dead of night, since anyone carrying three large
rubbish bags in daylight would look suspicious, to say the
least. The skull had rolled out when the bag had been
disturbed, probably by an animal, such as a dog or a rat
investigating the odorous package.

The bones contained in the other two bags were those of

a man 6 ft 1 in tall, who when alive had weighed some 180 pounds (approximately 13 stone). He had been between thirty-two and thirty-seven years of age, and had long, wavy black hair and a thick moustache. He had had extensive dental treatment, which would make identification easy if the dentist who had performed the work could be traced.

What most intrigued the police was the fact that the flesh had been carved from the larger bones by a sharp instrument such as a butcher's knife, and cut in such a manner as to suggest carving into joints like an animal carcase. Some of the bones had also been cut in half with what appeared to have been an electrically operated circular saw, and the marrow extracted with an implement which left impressions such as could have been made with a long-handled spoon with a narrow bowl. The head, and also some other body parts, appeared to have been kept in a deep-freeze or refrigerator prior to their having been dumped in the park.

Was there a cannibal at large in Münchengladbach?

The cause of death was impossible to determine, but it was clear that the victim had either died naturally or been murdered before being cut up for the pot. But before the police could do anything to catch such a ghoul, first of all the victim must be identified. The description of the man as he would have looked in life matched the description of the missing Josef Wirtz, but that was not enough: the dentist must be found who had attended to his teeth. A dental match would clinch the identification. So the police turned their attention to locating him. The chief of detectives in charge of the investigation assigned a contingent of officers to visit all local dentists with photographs of the victim's dental work, and before long they struck lucky. A dentist only a few hundred yards from the man's studio apartment recognized the dental work shown in the photographs as his own. The dentist was taken to the police morgue and shown the skull, and after examining the teeth he confirmed that the man had been one of his patients, a Josef Wirtz.

With the victim's identification now certain, the police

concentrated on looking for the perpetrator of the gruesome crime which had surfaced in their midst. First of all, the dead man's belongings were recovered from the basement of Herr Kreutzer's house and taken to police headquarters, where they were examined in detail on the off-chance of finding some clue to how he had met his fate. There were no black plastic rubbish bags among these items, but there were four other plastic bags. One was plain white and untraceable; a second bore the logo of a local supermarket, and it would of course be impossible to trace which one out of their thousands of customers had received it. The other two bags were, police thought, more promising. They were printed with the details of a video hire shop in the vicinity of the victim's address. The police thought that, possibly, it might be a good idea to try to trace the customers who had hired videos – especially horror films – during the period between Saturday, 2 June, when Wirtz had last been seen alive, and Monday, 4 June, when he had failed to report for work. It was thought that he had died – or been murdered – between those dates. And, possibly, a horror-film addict might have been responsible for the dismemberment.

The proprietor of the video hire shop produced a list of customers who had hired videos between the two dates in question. A customer wishing to hire a video had to give the proprietor his or her name and address and also a proof of identity, so obtaining such a list was straightforward. The police thanked the proprietor for his help and then immediately set about tracing all the individuals listed – quite an undertaking, since more than a hundred persons had rented videos over that weekend. To simplify their task, the police decided first to trace those who had rented horror films – the names of the films appeared beside their particulars so that the proprietor could keep tabs on who had borrowed what.

On 26 July two of the officers from this detail called at the fourth-floor apartment of Anna Martina Zimmermann, a 26-year-old mother of two young children aged six and four. The apartment building was not very far from the establishment owned by Herr Kreutzer. She was

separated from her husband, an unemployed carpenter
named Wilhelm Zimmermann. The woman ushered the
two detectives into the rather untidy living-room, which
was dominated by a large television set and a
free-standing bookcase containing rows of horror videos,
some her own and others rented from the hire shop. Anna
Zimmermann admitted freely she was a horror-film addict
– in fact she could scarcely deny it in the face of the
evidence. Asked whether she knew anyone named Josef
Wirtz, she admitted that she did, and that she knew he
was a barber.

While she was talking to one of the detectives, the other
was looking – seemingly casually – around her apartment.
In the kitchen, he found his attention drawn to the large
wooden table, which bore numerous bloodstains, as
though it was used regularly to cut up meat in quantity. It
was decided to take Frau Zimmermann to police
headquarters for further questioning.

The police chief leading the investigation at this point
decided to detail two other officers to search the
apartment while Frau Zimmermann was at headquarters
'helping with their inquiries'. Other officers were detailed
to find any witnesses in the apartment building who
might have seen anyone resembling Josef Wirtz entering
or leaving. And the welfare authorities were contacted for
a social worker to be appointed to look after Frau
Zimmermann's two small children while she was at police
headquarters. She had taken them there with her, since
they were too small to be left alone at the flat, and she had
no relatives or friends in Müchengladbach who could look
after them.

Frau Zimmermann was, by this time, becoming
distinctly nervous and refused to answer any further
questions except in the presence of a solicitor. As she did
not have one, the police summoned a lawyer on her
behalf, and he came to interview her in the detention cells.
He had just concluded his interview and was demanding
that the woman be released when the first reports from
the team searching her apartment began to come through.

The two detectives, who were still at the apartment, said

that they had discovered in the kitchen a large deep-freeze which contained forty or fifty plastic freezer boxes, many of which contained recognizable pieces of human flesh. There were human chops, joints and steaks, liver, heart, kidneys, and bones ostensibly for the making of soups or stock, as well as fat, not yet rendered, for cooking. Subsequent tests would confirm whether all this flesh was human, but pending such forensic examination it was clear that at least most of it was. Beef, lamb or pork does not have human fingers, ears, and other parts obviously belonging to the human male anatomy.

The police chief informed the solicitor of some of these findings, and the lawyer promptly abandoned his demands for Frau Zimmermann's release and went to conduct a further interview with her in the detention cell. He was still in the process of this interview when Frau Zimmermann's estranged husband, Wilhelm Zimmermann, was located and brought in for questioning in case he could shed any light on his wife's activities.

Informed that human flesh had been found in her deep-freeze, he offered no resistance to police questioning and declared himself ready to co-operate to the best of his ability. He admitted that he visited his wife from time to time and that on or about 2 June she had asked him to lend her an electric power-saw which she knew he had among his carpenter's tools. He complied – although he maintained that he did not know what she wanted to borrow it for. He presumed that she wanted it to cut wood for shelving or some other such DIY project.

Zimmermann stated that he knew Josef Wirtz, and knew that he was a friend of Anna's, although he had no evidence that they were lovers – Anna also denied this. As far as he was aware, her husband continued, Anna and Josef Wirtz's friendship was based mainly on an addiction to horror films, for which purpose they would both hire videos from the video shop. They would both sit watching the films for hours, until one day Wilhelm Zimmermann got fed up with the arrangement and moved out, mainly because he thought his wife was seeing too much of the handsome barber. He had no interest in horror films himself. This situation had been going on for almost two years before he left, but there comes a point when enough is enough, he added.

By now Anna Zimmermann had admitted killing Wirtz and cutting up his body on the kitchen table with the power-saw. Asked how she had killed him, she said that she had given him a glass of brandy laced with ground-up sleeping tablets. When he was in a drugged stupor, she assisted him to walk to the bathroom and pushed him head first into the bath. She then filled the bath with water and held his head under until he drowned. Her children had been happily playing in the next room.

She had purchased four dozen deep-freeze boxes all at once on Friday, 1 June, which would tend to indicate that the murder had been premeditated. She still had the receipt from the shop where she had purchased them. The head, bones and other parts that she considered inedible had been packed into plastic rubbish bags, which she had bundled into her younger child's pushchair and taken to the Bundgarten at 11 p.m. the same night, after first deep-freezing them to prevent blood leakage from the bags. At this point the pathologist who had examined the remains was asked to give his opinion as to why, if the bags had been in the park for as long as three or four weeks, they had not come to someone's attention sooner. His answer was that so long as the bags were tightly sealed no odours could escape, but as soon as a dog or other animal had loosened the string and the head had rolled out of its bag, odours would begin to permeate the atmosphere.

Anna Zimmermann astounded the police by stating that her sole motive for killing and dismembering Josef Wirtz was to obtain a supply of free meat. Her friendship with the deceased had had one main constituent – a mutual love of horror films of all kinds. Some had shown in gruesome detail how to dismember a dead body. This gave her the idea how to obtain a free meat supply. She did not work, and her husband, being unemployed, was unable to support her and the children. Meat is very expensive in Germany, and human flesh was reputed to taste like pork – a fact which she was able to corroborate from having tried it. Hardened police officers blanched as she launched into a detailed description of how to cook human tenderloin. They could scarcely believe this callous woman's story. And the worst thing was, in their eyes, the fact that the kitchen door had no lock and the young children, who slept and played in the adjoining room, could have come into the kitchen at any time.

Anna Zimmermann was charged with premeditated murder, but up to the time of writing she has never been brought to trial and is still under observation in a mental hospital to enable doctors to decide whether she is fit to stand trial. Her husband, who has consistently denied any involvement beyond lending his wife a power-saw in the belief that she wanted it for a DIY project, was charged with being an accessory. He will not come to trial until after a decision has been made as to whether his wife will appear in court on an indictment, and is still languishing in gaol.

6

Of Teeth and Gallstones

John George Haigh (1949)

Mrs Lane was understandably worried. Her close friend, Mrs Olivia Durand-Deacon, had not returned from a business trip which was most unlikely to have required more than an afternoon at most. Now it was the following day, already 9 a.m., and there was no sign of her. This was unprecendented; knowing her friend as she did, Mrs Lane knew that Olivia would just never have gone off or stayed the night somewhere else without telling her.

Mrs Lane and her friend were two elderly widows, both comfortably off, who lived at the Onslow Court Hotel, in Kensington, London. They had known each other for years and had both chosen the hotel as the place to spend their last days, living on the income from their stocks and shares and other investments. Mrs Durand-Deacon, in addition, still took an interest in small-business schemes, and it was one of these which had led to her half-day trip.

One of the hotel's male residents, John George Haigh, a dapper middle-aged businessman who never seemed to show any interest in women of his own age-group (or younger) but reserved his charm for rich elderly ladies, was a frequent visitor to the table in the dining-room which the two friends had reserved for their own use. He was a natty dresser with the gift of the gab, and always behaved with the utmost decorum – a trait which the two friends appreciated greatly. As one of them was later to say, 'John was always a gentleman.' It was therefore with no misgivings that Mrs Durand-Deacon took a considerable interest in what Haigh described as his latest new scheme for a money-spinner – the manufacture of plastic artificial fingernails in a small workshop he had in Crawley, Sussex – just a short train ride from London. Would she like to come and have a look at them and see some of his production methods? He, in his turn, was looking for one or two shareholders to help finance the product and launch it on the beauty market.

Mrs Durand-Deacon was delighted. It was just the kind of thing that appealed to her: no big financial outlay, and (Haigh said) a modest but steady return. Yes, she said, she would certainly like to visit his factory (as he called it). She would go that same afternoon – Friday, 18 February 1949. If they clinched the deal, Haigh said, he would take her out for a drink afterwards. So she went to her room to change, and came downstairs in her Persian lamb coat and some of her expensive jewellery, and carrying a red leather-look vinyl handbag.

At about six o'clock that evening Haigh returned to the hotel, and sought out Mrs Lane. 'Your friend did not turn up,' he told her. 'I waited an hour for her, but she did not come.'

'But I thought you were going to escort her on the train,' Mrs Lane replied.

'No, that was not the arrangement,' Haigh replied. 'I had to go there first to get things ready, and she would come later – she said she'd meet me at the factory at three o'clock. I gave her a piece of paper with a little map of how to get there.'

'Very odd,' Mrs Lane said. 'I wonder where she can have got to? It's not like her at all. Do you think she could have been taken ill or something like that along the way?'

'I really can't imagine – it's very odd, as you say,' Haigh replied. 'I'm sure, though, that if she'd been taken ill, someone would have let the hotel know. Let's see if she comes back later tonight. She might have taken it into her head to visit some other place in the neighbourhood – look round the shops or something of that kind.'

'But if she had changed her mind about the fingernail investment surely she would have met you to tell you,' Mrs Lane said. 'That would be only good manners. And she couldn't have got lost if you gave her a map of how to get to your factory.'

Mrs Lane was by now distinctly uneasy, but she kept her feelings to herself; her friend would doubtless return soon, with some reasonable explanation for her absence. She also checked with the hotel receptionist to see whether there had been any call from a hospital or doctor, but none such had been received. Did the suave, urbane John know anything about Olivia's disappearance? Was there something about this mystery which he knew but was keeping from her? Mrs Lane spent a sleepless night going over and over in her mind all the possible solutions.

At breakfast the following morning Haigh joined the visibly perplexed Mrs Lane at her table. 'I see your friend has not yet returned,' he said. 'What are we going to do?'

'I know what *I* am going to do,' Mrs Lane told him tersely. 'I am going to report her missing to the police.' She explained that it was completely out of character for Olivia to absent herself for so long without a word. Something untoward must have happened to her, she added, firmly convinced in her own mind that this was the only possible explanation.

'I will go with you,' offered Haigh. 'I might be able to help.' Mrs Lane agreed, and after the meal they set off together for the nearby Chelsea Police Station, where a woman officer, Sergeant Lambourne, took details and was appointed to investigate the mystery. It is on record that she 'distrusted Haigh on sight'; whether this was due to her extensive experience of dealing with criminals or just feminine intuition is not clear, though it was probably a combination of both. This feeling was confirmed when she interviewed the hotel manager, who informed her that Haigh was invariably slow at paying his bill.

Meanwhile Haigh made a number of visits to his so-called factory, and his comings and goings were discreetly watched by police officers in plain clothes and unmarked cars. Nothing unusual was observed about his behaviour; he was merely a businessman visiting his workshop. It was ascertained that the building, which Haigh grandly called his factory, was a disused warehouse let to him by a firm called Hurst Lea Products, with an office in Leopold Road, Crawley. The warehouse was situated at the back of the office, screened from it by a high wooden fence and set well back from the main road.

Detective Inspector Shelley Symes, who was in charge of the case, visited Haigh at the Onslow Court Hotel and questioned him closely regarding what he could tell the police about the missing woman. Dissatisfied with Haigh's glib, self-assured manner and his statements about the unkept appointment, Symes decided that Haigh's Crawley workshop should be searched in case any possible clues came to light. The search was carried out without Haigh's knowledge. In it they found a .38 Webley revolver and eight rounds of ammunition hidden in an old dust-covered hat-box on a shelf, as well as a dry-cleaning firm's docket for a Persian lamb coat issued by the firm's Reigate branch. Symes knew that the missing woman had been wearing such a coat when she disappeared. Among items found in the workshop ostensibly for use in some kind of manufacturing process were three large carboys of concentrated sulphuric acid, rubber protective clothing, and face masks such as are used by factory workers to avoid inhaling toxic fumes. Symes, a very observant detective, also spotted faint traces of blood on one of the walls.

On the detective inspector's return to headquarters, he was informed that a report had just come in that Mrs Durand-Deacon's jewellery had been sold to a shop in Horsham for £100 and her gold watch pawned for £50 at the same establishment. These transactions had taken place on Saturday, 19 February – the day after the widow's disappearance. It was noted that the dry-cleaners' ticket was also dated 19 February. It was also observed that in both cases Haigh had given his correct name, but a different address, in Pimlico. It was quickly established that Haigh had been a firewatcher at that address during the war.

At 4.15 p.m. on 28 February Haigh was seen at the Onslow Court Hotel and taken into custody at Chelsea Police Station. Questioned once more about his knowledge of the whereabouts of Mrs Durand-Deacon, he changed his story several times and was evasive on a number of points.

But the police did not believe him, and told him so. Symes left the suspect in the detention room with Detective Inspector Albert Webb while he (Symes) conferred with senior officers. Haigh appeared to become very uneasy and nervous. 'Tell me, officer,' he asked, 'what are the chances of anyone being released from Broadmoor?'

Webb declined to answer, but privately he no doubt thought that they were about nil. 'Well,' Haigh continued, 'if I told you the truth you wouldn't believe me.'

At this point Symes returned with another officer and Haigh was cautioned. He shrugged nonchalantly and replied, 'Yes, I know all that. I will tell you all about it. Mrs Durand-Deacon has disappeared completely, and no trace of her will ever be found.'

'How do you make that out?' said Webb. 'What has happened to her, then?'

'I have destroyed her completely with acid. Every trace has gone. You will find the sludge at my factory in Leopold Road. How can you prove murder without a body?'

Haigh was wrong on both counts. First of all, the prosecution has to prove that murder has been committed, not produce the body; secondly, forensic experts were later to be able to prove that Mrs Durand-Deacon had not been *completely* destroyed ...

Charged with the murder of Mrs Olivia Durand-Deacon, Haigh's confession came in the form of a statement which he dictated to DI Shelley Symes – a statement which took all of two and a half hours to write.

He admitted that his story of an unkept appointment was false. He had driven Mrs Durand-Deacon to Crawley in his car. He showed her the plastic fingernails, in which she was taking a keen interest, and while she was bending over the bench on which they were displayed to look at them more closely, he shot her in the back of the head with the .38. After removing her Persian lamb fur coat, her gold watch and the pearls and diamonds she was wearing, he managed to haul up her fully clothed body and hoist it into a forty-gallon steel tank. This must have been quite a feat, for Haigh was not very tall, and Mrs Durand-Deacon weighed a hefty fourteen stone. After this prodigious effort, Haigh nipped across the road to the Old Priory Café, where he partook of a poached egg on toast and a cup of tea.

Returning to the workshop, he had pumped concentrated sulphuric acid into the tank with a stirrup-pump until the body was completely covered. He then removed the protective clothing he had put on, had a good wash, and went off to the George Hotel not far away for dinner. He had then driven back home to Onslow Court.

Three days later, calculating that the dissolving of the body would by then be complete, he returned to the workshop to examine his grisly handiwork. After skimming off some fat which had floated to the surface and dumping it on the ground outside, he pumped more acid into the tank. The following day he considered it safe to empty the tank, and poured the sludge out on to the ground outside. By that time he had realized the sale of the jewellery and was able to pay £50 arrears of rent to Mr Jones, the manager of Hurst Lea Products, who rented the workshop to him.

At this point, Chief Inspector Guy Mahon took charge of the case, and arranged for a team of forensic scientists, headed by Professor Keith Simpson, to be driven in a police car to the Leopold Road workshop in Crawley to examine the sludge to which Haigh had referred in his statement. The land outside the building consisted of rough waste ground, mainly earth and small pebbles. The sludge covered an area of about six feet by four feet, and lay on the surface three or four inches deep. It was a messy, odorous and unpleasant task indeed to scrape up this substance and transfer it into metal tanks for transport to the Metropolitan Police Forensic Science Laboratory.

While Professor Simpson was looking round outside the building, paying attention to the pebbles and earth at the edge of the sludge-covered area, he noticed one pebble that was more rounded than the rest, about the size of a cherry, with smoothly polished facets. Simpson picked it up, examined it more closely through a magnifying-glass and realized that it was a gallstone. Later laboratory tests proved that it was in fact a human gallstone – a malady which often afflicts plump ladies of seventy like Mrs Durand-Deacon who are partial to rich food, good wine and not too much exercise. The fatty substance with which gallstones are covered resists the dissolving action of the stomach acids – and sulphuric acid.

For the next three days Professor Simpson, assisted by Dr H.S. Holden and under the watchful eye of Superintendent Cuthbert of Scotland Yard, examined the sludge, spread out thinly on a number of shallow steel trays to facilitate analysis. Two more human gallstones were found, as well as fragments of human bone that had escaped dissolution but were much eroded; these included parts of the bones of a female left foot. There was evidence of some degree of osteoarthritis in the joints of some of the bone fragments found, which pointed to the victim having been elderly. Other finds including a red handbag handle made of acid-resistant plastic, and a metal lipstick case. Finally, a complete set of dentures was found. False teeth, as well as natural ones, have to be acid-resistant if they are going to be used when consuming acidic foods; after all, they would be little use otherwise. Haigh had certainly not done his homework – and this was to be his undoing.

As if all this were not enough, Professor Simpson reconstructed a left foot from the bones he had found, and this fitted exactly into one of the dead woman's left shoes.

Miss Helen Mayo, who had been Mrs Durand-Deacon's dentist, was quickly found. She stated that she had supplied the dentures about eighteen months previously, and they were, she said, without any doubt the ones she had fitted in September 1947.

* * *

Meantime Haigh, asked to sign his statement, told the police that he could not sign it just yet – he hadn't finished. There was more to come – much more.

In 1943, he continued in his confession, he rented a basement workroom at 79 Gloucester Road, Kensington, where he worked, as he said, on various 'inventive manufacturing procedures'. At about this time he met a man named Donald McSwann, who was the proprietor of a chain of amusement arcades. The McSwann family were quite well off, owning houses in Wimbledon, Raynes Park and Beckenham as well as having a sizeable bank balance. Haigh inveigled McSwann into coming to his workshop on some pretext, and once he was inside he bludgeoned him to death with a cosh, and dissolved his body in a vat of acid. This took place on 9 September 1944, and when the acid had done its job Haigh poured its contents down the drain. This time there were no tell-tale gallstones or teeth ...

Haigh had been quite friendly with the McSwann family, and it was common knowledge that Donald was trying to dodge the call-up. This situation, he mused, had distinct possibilities. When Donald's parents called on Haigh to find out of he had any knowledge of the whereabouts of their missing son, he told them that Donald had had to go into hiding in Scotland to escape the army authorities, and that he (Haigh) had been given a power of attorney to manage Donald's amusement arcade business in his absence. The elder McSwann insisted on seeing the alleged power of attorney, and called at Haigh's workshop. Three ten-gallon carboys of fresh sulphuric acid were waiting to convert him.

Some time later that evening, Mrs McSwann, anxious to know why her husband had not returned from his visit to Haigh, decided to find out, and met a similar fate. Haigh did not say in his confession how he had killed the couple. He went on to say that, with a skilfully forged power of attorney, he obtained control of Donald's business and sold all the pin-tables and gambling machines, and re-let the arcades to other franchises. He then forged equally skilfully a power of attorney over the elder McSwanns' property, and thereby obtained real property worth about £10,000, which he promptly sold, plus the bank balance of a little over £4,000.

Three years later, in 1947, he struck up a friendship with a Dr and Mrs Henderson, whom he had met during the course of a property deal. The deal itself did not proceed, but the three of them became boon companions. By February of the following year Haigh was in need of cash, and decided that Dr Archibald Henderson and his wife Rosalie would make ideal victims, since they were financially well placed, with property readily obtainable by 'power of attorney'.

By this time Haigh had given up the Gloucester Road workshop and rented the one in Crawley, and it was here that he lured Dr Henderson, on the pretext of showing him round his 'factory'. Dr Henderson was shot in the back of the head while he was bending to look at some object on a bench. The doctor was tall and slender and would have been much less trouble to get into a tank of acid than the corpulent Mrs Durand-Deacon at a later date.

Haigh was in no mood to hang about until Mrs Henderson called at his premises to look for her husband as time passed. Instead, he telephoned her at home and informed her that her husband had been taken ill – would she please come immediately? She did.

From the unfortunate Hendersons Haigh gained almost £8,000 – his skill at forgery was such that banks, solicitors, anyone who examined these documents, could not fault them.

To conclude his statement, Haigh stated that he had drunk the blood of all his victims, which was a preposterous claim. His sole motive for the murders was pecuniary gain. As a battery of expert psychiatrists who later examined him were to point out, Haigh had no perversions or even very much in the way of sexuality at all. His absurd claims were drummed up simply to try to convince the doctors that he was insane and would thus be spared the death penalty. He concocted wild fantasies such as that he had nightmares about forests dripping blood, and even drank his own urine in prison so that the warders would consider him a nutcase. His chances of being released from Broadmoor? He would never go there. He was not mad according to the law, but legally sane.

He even invented three further murders, which were

non-existent, saying that these were committed from blood lust and not for money. Balderdash, said the police; poppycock, echoed the doctors. He was quickly shown up for the sham he was.

In the meantime the police had not been slow to check up in the Criminal Records Office to see whether Haigh had a record. They were not in the least surprised. At the age of twenty-one he was sentenced to fifteen months' imprisonment on charges of obtaining money under false pretences by means of a hire-purchase swindle. After his release he moved to a south-coast town and set up practice as a bogus solicitor, and managed to defraud his clients of more than £30,000 by selling non-existent stocks and shares. This netted him four years' penal servitude.

All this prison did not deter him, however. After coming out of Dartmoor in 1940, at the age of thirty-one, he burgled evacuated houses and in the following year he was caught and sentenced to twenty-one months' hard labour. He was released in 1943.

'I told you so!' said Police Sergeant Lambourne at Chelsea Police Station – the policewoman who had sniffed out the bogus 'businessman' as a ferret sniffs out a rabbit.

* * *

The trial was truly a *cause célèbre*, the Attorney General, Sir Hartley Shawcross, leading for the Crown, and the defence being conducted by Sir David Maxwell Fyfe (later Lord Kilmuir), a future Lord Chancellor. The judge was Sir Travers Humphreys, eighty-one years old at the time. The trial was held in the Lewes (Sussex) Assize Court.

The court was packed, and the streets around literally besieged, on the day of the trial, 18 July 1949. The trial ended the same day, after thirty-three witnesses had been called, because only four of them were cross-examined. Maxwell Fyfe called only one witness, Dr Henry Yellowlees, a psychiatrist, who strove valiantly to try to prove that Haigh was insane. Two other eminent psychiatrists had examined Haigh in Brixton Prison, but the non-committal tone of the reports from these two had discouraged the defence from calling them.

The prosecution called several distinguished psychiatrists to refute the opinion of Dr Yellowlees, who was unable, despite his impressive array of degrees and academic honours, even to begin to make his diagnosis of paranoia stick. The prosecution's expert witnesses soon demolished this theory and were easily able to prove that Haigh's so-called 'symptoms' were no more than a calculated attempt to simulate insanity.

The jury were equally unimpressed by the insanity plea and were out for only a quarter of an hour before returning a unanimous verdict of guilty. Haigh was executed at Wandsworth Prison on 6 August.

It is of interest to note that, long before Haigh's trial, shock, horror and excitement ran high over this series of callous murders, and one newspaper, the *Daily Mirror*, was not slow to capitalize on Haigh's more lurid confessions, which somehow had been leaked to them. 'The Vampire Killer' was the theme of the banner headlines, with descriptions of Haigh's alleged blood-drinking orgies and other 'confessions'. The *Mirror* was quickly taken to task for contempt of court, the newspaper being fined £10,000 and its editor, Silvester Bolam, sentenced to three months in Brixton, the same prison where Haigh had been held.

It is chilling to think what might have happened if Haigh's crimes had been committed today; the television reporters would have had a field day – and probably a few writs would have come their way in due course.

7

The John Barleycorn Murder

Harold Loughans (1944)

The John Barleycorn is a public house in Portsmouth, Hampshire, and in 1943 the proprietress was a Mrs Rose Ada Robinson, a 63-year-old widow. She had run the pub successfully for forty years, and lived in the flat above. She employed a permanent barman named John Welch, and several part-time and temporary barmen and barmaids.

Mrs Robinson was well respected and kept an eminently decent establishment, but she had one failing – more an eccentric habit than anything, but one which was to prove her undoing: she mistrusted banks. It was her custom to clear the till every night after closing-time and put the money into two large, old, black leather handbags which had seen better days. These she would stow into a cupboard in her bedroom. Admittedly the cupboard did have a lock, but it was a very flimsy sort of affair and a child could have broken into it with a penknife – to quote a police officer's later comments. Unfortunately for Mrs Robinson, it had become common knowledge that she kept the cash locked up in her bedroom. One can only conjecture how this information could have leaked out.

On the night of 28 November Mrs Robinson rang 'Time, gentlemen, please' earlier than usual, for it was a Sunday. John Welch closed the bar and locked up the premises, while Mrs Robinson took the cash from the till and put it into her two battered old handbags. Business had been good – the takings came to £450. Very pleased with herself, the old lady said good-night to the barman and went up to her flat to bed. The last thing she heard was

Welch slamming the door as he left to go home. The door was self-locking without a key.

The following morning Welch came to open and prepare for the day's trade. He had a key to the door to enter, although no key was, as we have seen, needed to leave. He was mildly surprised to note that Mrs Robinson was not around, which was unusual for her – it was, after all, ten o'clock. He decided to give her a quarter of an hour and, if she had not appeared by then, to go up to the flat and knock at the door. She was, after, getting on a bit – and, you never know, she could have had a heart attack or something.

Welch knocked at the door of the flat, but there was no answer. He knocked again, with the same result. He tried the door and found, much to his surprise, that he was able to push it open. It was unprecedented for Mrs Robinson to leave the door of her flat unlocked. Was she ill? He called out her name, but there was no reply. Emboldened by fear, he walked into the flat. There was no sign of her about. The kitchen was neat and tidy and there was no coffee pot bubbling or breakfast dishes laid out, or washing-up left in the sink. Very odd.

Convinced by now that his employer had been taken seriously ill in the night, Welch went to the bedroom, gave a perfunctory knock – again eliciting no response – and entered. The room had been ransacked, with clothing and other items strewn all over the floor, drawers pulled out of chests and upended, cupboard and wardrobe doors open. The two old black handbags lay on the floor, ripped open and empty. Mrs Robinson lay face upwards on the bed. She was very obviously dead, staring with sightless eyes at the ceiling. Welch did not stop to look further but, his heart pounding, rushed downstairs and called the police.

Shortly after 10 a.m. the police arrived. The pathologist, Dr Keith Simpson, whom we met in the last chapter, examined the body briefly prior to the autopsy which he would perform later, and stated that Mrs Robinson had been dead for seven or eight hours. This tied in with the statement of the next-door neighbour, who said he had been disturbed by noises coming from the premises between two and three o'clock in the morning.

On the ground floor the police found a rear window broken, to which the catch had been forced, and an unbolted and unlocked back door, from which they deduced, correctly, that the intruder had entered by the window and left by the door. The entire flat was dusted for fingerprints, but the burglar had either worn gloves or had wiped clean any fingerprints; the only ones found were those of the old lady herself. A small black button with a broken thread attached, probably from a man's jacket, was found on the window-ledge below the window which had been broken to gain entry to the flat.

The blackout curtain at the bedroom window had been pulled to one side, as though the intruder needed more light but wished to avoid calling attention to his presence by switching on the electric light, though doubtless he used a torch. The burglar must have been aware of the fact that Mrs Robinson kept large sums of money in her bedroom instead of taking them to the bank. No other items had been stolen from the room, which had obviously been ransacked until the two handbags had come to light.

Mrs Robinson had been strangled. It would seem that she had been awakened by the noise as the burglar entered, and had been silenced to stop her raising the alarm. Dr Simpson found a deep bruise on the right-hand side of the larynx (voice-box), which appeared to have been made by the pressure of a thumb, and three much lighter bruises in a straight line on the other side. Dr Simpson was struck by the fact that these three – presumably finger impressions – were so much lighter than the thumb-mark. Had the murderer been a *woman*? The only snag in this theory was that the line of finger impressions was four inches across – rather large for a woman's hand. Still, a tall woman could have large hands. The murderer – whether he or she – was right-handed. Another curious feature of these marks was that there were no curved fingernail impressions as usually appeared in a manual strangling. Several scratches were apparent on the neck, which Dr Simpson considered were not made by the murderer but had been caused by Mrs

Robinson herself as she struggled ineffectively to prise off the hand, or hands, which gripped her neck, slowly strangling her to death. There were certainly signs of a struggle, with bedclothes in disarray and pillows awry.

Police made strenuous efforts to find the person who had snuffed out the life of the old lady for the £450 she had in those two black bags, but the days passed into weeks and they were no nearer a solution, although they had managed to trace everyone who had been in the John Barleycorn that night and interviewed all of them.

* * *

Almost a month after the unsolved murder, two plain-clothes detective constables were patrolling a seedy area of south-east London on the lookout for thieves who had been giving them a lot of trouble with repeated petty crimes. Someone, they knew – possibly more than one person – was 'fencing' stolen property on quite a regular scale, and almost every day fresh complaints were coming in of property missing.

After all the footslogging involved, the two officers felt that they could do with a well-earned cup of tea. So they turned into a sleazy-looking transport café in the Waterloo Road. While the waitress was taking their order, they noticed a shabbily dressed middle-aged man behaving in a furtive manner. It seemed he was trying to sell a new pair of men's shoes to the lorry-drivers and other folk who frequented the café. A barrow-boy from the local market started to take an interest in the bargain, and at this point the two officers forgot their tea and took the shabby man with the shoes in for questioning. He turned out to be Harold Loughans, an old lag with plenty of 'form' – he had spent more years in prison than he had on the outside.

In the police van Loughans became very talkative. 'These shoes are nothing,' he said. 'I nicked them from a house in Bermondsey. But I'm wanted for things far more serious than this, though. The Yard wants me. It's the trapdoor for me now.'

The officers let him babble on. 'I'm glad you picked me

up,' the ex-con continued. 'It'll do you good.' While still in the police van, he produced from his coat pocket a silver cigarette-box. 'There's a nice Christmas box for you,' he said as he handed the box to one of the officers. 'I know this will be my last Christmas.'

On arrival at Kennington Road Police Station, the garrulous prisoner kept on talking. Nothing, it seems, not even a caution, could stem the tide. 'I'm glad I've been nicked,' he said. 'I've been through hell these last three weeks. I've been a bastard all my life, but I never knocked anybody off before. I was sorry the moment I done the job – I haven't slept a wink since. It has preyed on my mind. She must've had a weak heart, the poor old girl.'

After giving his name, Harold Loughans was again cautioned, and carried on talking relentlessly. 'It's a relief to get it off my mind,' he said. 'I had to stop her screaming, but I didn't mean to kill her. You know what it's like when a woman starts screaming.' Asked who 'she' was, he admitted: 'I want to say I done that murder at the pub in Portsmouth three or four weeks ago. I know this is the end of the road for me. I deserve all I get.' Loughans put his head in his hands and sobbed unrestrainedly.

His contrition seemed genuine enough, but it did not excuse a most brutal crime against a defenceless old lady.

'Where did you get the silver cigarette-case?' an officer asked.

'It was when I done a job in St Albans last week,' Loughans replied. 'I tied a woman to a bed and hit her on the head with my torch to shut her up. I got the cigarette-case and some other stuff from there.'

'Do you say that you still committed burglaries and robbery with violence even after you had killed the old lady at the John Barleycorn?' one of the interrogating officers queried.

'Yes. I done about a dozen jobs since then – Mill Hill, Edgware, other places I can't remember the names of. It was to get the big job off my mind.'

Loughans was then asked to make a written statement, which he dictated to a police officer. He admitted that he had heard about Mrs Robinson's habit of keeping the pub takings in her flat from another regular. But he had not been drinking in the pub on the night he committed the crime. He was not a regular habitué of the pub, but had visited it while on a look round the town to assess its prospects for burglaries.

There were no buttons on his coat or his jacket that matched the one that had been found on the window-ledge at the scene of the crime, but all his clothing was sent to the Metropolitan Police Laboratory. Forensic scientists there found a few items that could, possibly, be tied in with the fact of his having been in the room where the murder had been committed: a hemp fibre on one boot that could have come from the doormat there; a green wool fibre which was identical with those in a green rug in the bedroom; and feathers from a quilt. These finds were not in themselves forensically conclusive; thousands of similar doormats were made of hemp fibre and green wool rugs, even of the same make, could be found practically anywhere. As for the feathers, these formed the filling of thousands of quilts; synthetic material for quilt fillings had not yet become common. More telling, however, was a bloodstain found on the inner side of the cuff of the suspect's jacket. Experts dated it as about three to four weeks old.

If the police had had only these slender clues to go on, the evidence against Loughans to substantiate his confession might have been thin indeed. But there was another factor which clinched the case against Loughans. He had a deformed right hand, his four fingers being only half-length stumps, with no nails. The thumb was normal.

Dr Simpson was quick to spot the connection between this feature of Loughan's right hand and the appearance of the strangulation bruises on the deceased woman's neck. The thumbprint was quite normal, but if Loughans had indeed strangled Mrs Robinson, the impressions of the four fingers – weaker and devoid of nailprints – would have been exactly similar to those actually presenting at the autopsy.

The trial of Harold Loughans took place in March 1944 at Winchester Assizes. Mr J.D. Casswell prosecuted, and Loughans was defended by Mr John Maude.

In the dock Loughans showed his deformed right hand to the jury, pointing out that it was too weak to enable him to strangle anybody. 'I could not even strangle a cat with a hand like that,' he said. He repudiated his confessions, alleging that they had been fabricated by the police. Mr Maude made the point that the Portsmouth police had corrected some inaccuracies in the accused's statement to the Metropolitan Police officers who had arrested him and who had not had the same knowledge of the details of the crime.

Mr Maude's ace card, however, which came as a complete surprise to the court, took the form of four witnesses who all swore that Loughans had spent the entire night of the murder sleeping on the platform in Warren Street Tube Station in London, which was being used as an air-raid shelter. All four witnesses identified Loughans by his deformed right hand, and did not know him personally.

Mr Casswell, the prosecutor, was unable to shake any of these witnesses, and naturally the police had not had any time at all to investigate Loughan's alibi. In the end, the jury failed to reach agreement, and the judge ordered a re-trial.

By the time the new trial took place two weeks later at the Old Bailey, the police had collected what they considered to be evidence in rebuttal of the accused's alibi, but the judge would not allow this to be admitted, stating that it should have been properly presented at the first trial. At this new trial Mr Maude challenged Dr Keith Simpson's evidence about Loughan's hand in which he averred that even with this deformity the accused could very well have strangled someone. He also pointed out that if a strangler had worn gloves no nail impressions would have been made. Then, to the astonishment of the court, Maude produced his final trump card.

'Call Sir Bernard Spilsbury!' he announced in a dramatic voice worthy of any stage performance.

The court stirred visibly, a great wave of speculation running through the Old Bailey like a tidal undertow. What was Sir Bernard doing here for the defence? Almost always, the great man appeared for the prosecution. Dr Simpson was plainly bemused. He knew that Spilsbury had not seen the dead body, nor even the forensic report in his (Simpson's) laboratory. What could he say?

The court was soon to be enlightened. Spilsbury had visited Loughans in Brixton Prison at the instigation of the defence, and had asked the prisoner to grip his hand, as in shaking hands, with as much strength as he could muster. For a man faced with a capital charge, one can readily visualize the situation. Loughans put up a most creditable performance in an effort to escape the hangman's noose. Now, in court, the flabbergasted prosecution heard no less a personage than the famous Sir Bernard himself tell them of the limp, flabby handshake he had received from Harold Loughans. 'I do not believe that he could strangle anyone with that hand,' he said.

Casswell was clearly put out. He tried in vain to persuade Sir Bernard to admit the possibility that his judgement had erred on the side of allowing Loughans the benefit of the doubt – in other words, suggesting that he might have allowed himself, albeit unwittingly, to be hoodwinked by the prisoner into believing that there was less strength in his deformed hand than he knew to be the case.

Spilsbury looked at the prosecutor in utter incredulity at such a suggestion – a look which plainly challenged Casswell's temerity in implying that Sir Bernard could be wrong or that his judgement could be impaired by the age and infirmity which had crept up on him as he neared the end of his brilliant career. Counsel and senior police officers alike perhaps remembered a memorable utterance by Casswell fourteen years earlier at the trial of Sidney Fox in 1930:[1] 'It will be a sorry day for the administration of criminal justice in this land if we are to be thrust into such a position that, because Sir Bernard Spilsbury expressed an opinion, it is of such weight that it is impossible to question it.'

Sir Bernard drew himself up to his full height. 'Certainly not!' he snapped.

The charisma of Spilsbury's reputation was too much

for the jury. Loughans was acquitted without further ado.

* * *

Loughans, doubtless rejoicing that he was walking free from the Old Bailey, was in for a nasty shock. Outside the court police officers were waiting to arrest him for a robbery with violence he had committed in Edgware, in which he had tied an old woman to a chair with wire, nearly killing her. He was convicted and sent to prison. This did not stop him, however, for after his release he committed another violent crime, hitting a woman on the head and tying her up as she lay unconscious, while he ransacked her flat and walked out with all her money and jewellery. Two boys spotted him making his getaway across some gardens and dialled 999. This time he was given fifteen years' preventive detention.

By the time he came out of prison in 1963 – almost twenty years after the John Barleycorn murder – he was a broken man, almost seventy years of age. Burglarly had lost its appeal for him, so he did the next best thing – he wrote his memoirs for the *People* newspaper, who probably paid him considerably more than he would have gained from burglary. At the end of the article he admitted that he had in fact strangled Mrs Robinson at the John Barleycorn pub. He was photographed by the *People* signing his confession, holding the pen in his deformed right hand.

Three months later Harold Loughans was dead.

Note

1. Georgina Lloyd, *With Malice Aforethought* (Robert Hale, 1989).

8

A Skeleton in the Cupboard

Sarah Jane Harvey (1960)

Leslie Harvey had been a good son, no doubt about it. After his father had died in 1938, he lived in his mother's house for the next twenty years, looking after her. Being a self-employed taxi-driver, he was able to plan his hours of work so that he could give his mother the care she needed. For many years she had been in very frail health – lame from disseminated sclerosis and also suffering from a chronic kidney disease. But she usually managed to keep a brave face on things. Although she had to walk with a stick, she was never heard to complain about the pain, and was known for her sense of humour and cheerful expression. Leslie was a dab hand at DIY and did all manner of odd jobs for her, including carpentry, plumbing repairs and the usual restorative needs of an old house.

In 1958 Leslie married and went to live in Abergele, not far from Rhyl, the North Wales town where he had lived until then. His mother continued to live at 35 Kinmel Street, the modest two-storeyed terraced house which had been their home.

Mrs Sarah Jane Harvey's income had been from lodgers, a succession of whom had stayed in the little house and partaken of Mrs Harvey's substantial Welsh cooking. She kept the house spotless, and no lodgers were ever known to have any complaints. One of these ladies, a Mrs Frances Alice Knight, had been the wife of a well-known dentist, who had left her in 1936. She did not bother with a divorce, but, wishing to stay in her home town, took a room in Mrs Harvey's establishment, while her husband had gone to live in Hove, near Brighton in Sussex. He paid her the weekly sum of £2 maintenance ordered by the court, in addition to which Mrs Knight had her old-age pension. She paid Mrs Harvey thirty shillings a week for her room and board.

In April 1960 Mrs Harvey's health took a turn for the worse: cancer was suspected. She was, after all, sixty-five and, as we have seen, already crippled with disseminated sclerosis and frequently incapacitated by a kidney complaint. Mrs Harvey was admitted into hospital for observation and tests. As these procedures would take some time, Leslie considered it a good opportunity for him to redecorate her home in readiness for when she would be discharged. The house was still in good order, thanks to his having looked after it for so many years, but the woodwork could do with a new coat of paint, and several of the rooms would be made brighter and more attractive with new wallpaper. Leslie still had his own key, of course, so he went round to the house, with his wife, one evening to measure up for the number of rolls of wallpaper and cans of paint he would require to do the job.

Leaving his wife to look around downstairs, Leslie climbed the stairs to the first-floor landing, and the first thing that met his eyes was the two-door pinewood cupboard which extended from ceiling to floor. It had always been kept locked, as it was now, and it had aroused his curiosity ever since he had been a boy. Once his mother had caught him fiddling with the lock and given him a good telling-off. 'There's stuff stored in there that belongs to those London folks who lodged here during the blitz,' she had later explained. 'They will come and pick it up one of these days and will carry on alarming if they think anybody's been meddling with it.'

Leslie had come to accept this explanation for a long time, but now he decided to investigate. After all, it was at least twenty years ago, and nobody had ever come to claim their belongings. He took a large screwdriver from his tool kit and forced the lock. A wave of fetid air assailed him as he pushed the doors open. Hanging flypapers and dusty cobwebs obscured his view. He took a small plumber's torch from the kit and shone its beam through the obstruction. He saw what looked like a mouldering blanket, with a withered, brown human foot and lower leg protruding from beneath it. 'My God,' he said aloud, slamming the doors shut.

'What is it?' his wife called from downstairs.

Leslie ran downstairs. 'It's a body!' he gasped, visibly shaken.

'A *body*?' his wife cried. 'Where?'

'In that locked cupboard on the landing,' he said. 'We'll go round to your father's – we can call the police from there.' Leslie and his wife went straight round to the house, which was only a few streets away, and the two men agreed that they should both go and look more closely at the contents of the cupboard before informing the police. It would not do at all to drag the police into it if they proved, after all, to be mistaken and what looked like a body was only a bundle of old clothes and blankets. The 'leg' could, in that dim light, have been only a old boot.

A small plumber's torch, with its narrow spotlight beam, was inadequate to light up the dark interior of the cupboard, but Leslie's father-in-law had a Tilley lamp in his garden shed, which would throw a wide circle of light into the gloom. The two men took the lamp and made their way to 35 Kinmel Street. It took little more than a cursory examination to realize that it was not just somebody's possessions in that cupboard – it was *somebody* ...

* * *

Police were soon in Kinmel Street, and by late evening Reginald Atkins, the Chief Constable of Flintshire, accompanied by the coroner, Dr Rhys Llewellyn Jones, were taking a much closer look at the remains than either Leslie Harvey or his father-in-law had, quite understandably, wished to do. The body was in a doubled-up position, probably to enable the person who had put it there to cram it into the somewhat confined space. The clothing, though grimy, faded and cobweb-encrusted, was still recognizable as a nightdress and dressing-gown. The remnants of what appeared to be a lisle stocking were also found around the neck. The body itself was little more than a skeleton, and what flesh remained was shrunken and leathery, and as hard as stone. The skeleton in the cupboard was in fact perhaps better described as a mummy.

The preservation of the body had been achieved by the agency of warm, dry air rising and circulating around the cupboard tomb, gradually desiccating the tissues. This had enabled the body to remain concealed for many years without giving rise to the tell-tale odour of decomposition. Called to view the corpse in an effort to ascertain its identity, Leslie Harvey was able to state that the now hideous death-mask bore some faint resemblance to a lodger named Mrs Knight who had lodged at the house some twenty years earlier. As he recalled, if his memory served him rightly, his mother had said she had left some time in 1940. Why should anyone have wanted to keep her dead body in the cupboard for twenty years, even going to the trouble of hanging flypapers in the space above the corpse with the obvious intention of keeping insect infestation at bay? Leslie Harvey could give the police no clues, although he had lived in the house until 1958.

Dr Edward Gerald Evans was the pathologist called upon to perform the post-mortem. The removal of the body from the cupboard had been a most difficult and indeed nauseating task, since every time it was moved clouds of dust rose, choking the police officers engaged in this task. Cobwebs, dead flies, dead spiders and rotting clothes all added to the unpleasantness of the job.

The corpse was seen to be that of an elderly woman about 5 ft 4 in tall. The fact that she had limped was indicated by differing leg lengths caused by disease; indeed it was correctly deduced that she had been in the last stages of disseminated sclerosis. Other examination techniques disclosed that she had been right-handed, was probably about sixty-five years of age, and had most likely had Group A blood. The ravages of time had destroyed most of the hair, the teeth, the internal organs and even the blood-vessels; it was, however, postulated that the absence of teeth might have been due to the victim's having worn dentures which she had removed. It takes a very long time and a lot of decay to destroy teeth so completely.

Generations of maggots – fly larvae – had taken their toll, however, despite the provision of flypapers. So had broods of clothes-moth grubs. It was these which would have eaten the hair as well as the garments in which the body had been clothed, leaving them in tattered remnants.

The most significant discovery of all, however, was a groove around the neck, which pathologists ascertained had been caused by a ligature – in other words, the victim had been strangled. So now what the doctors and the police were looking at was not a body that had been hidden after dying a natural death, but murder.

It is one thing to say that someone has been murdered, but quite another to find out who committed the murder, especially after an interval of twenty years. It was also a puzzle to find the motive. Who would want to murder a little old lady and then keep her body in a cupboard for such a long time? The police realized from the outset that they had a mammoth task on their hands, but they did not let the obvious drawbacks of time-lapse and a dearth of clues deter them.

Detective Inspector Hugh Williams and Detective Sergeant William Evans were detailed to try to ascertain any link between the dead woman and Mrs Knight, based on Leslie Harvey's suspicion that it was she whose remains had been found. First of all, the two detectives visited the registry office in St Asaph to find out whether there was any record of the death of Mrs Knight. No such record existed and no death certificate had been issued. But even more revelations were to come. On visiting the Rhyl municipal offices, an official informed them that he certainly knew Mrs Knight and that she lived at 35 Kinmel Street; he told the two officers that her landlady was a Mrs Harvey, who had been collecting her lodger's maintenance cheque and pension for the last twenty years because Mrs Knight was housebound!

The police officers look at one another in disbelief. So that was the motive – Mrs Harvey had murdered her lodger for her weekly allowances! The money had been unfailingly collected each week by Mrs Harvey in person, who had at the beginning produced what purported to be Mrs Knight's written authority to collect it on her behalf, owing to chronic ill-health which left her bedridden. The staff of the Magistrates' Clerk's office had accepted this document as genuine and handed over the money without question, and later when Mrs Knight had attained the age to draw her pension, Mrs Harvey had used the same method to collect this from the post office, again without question. Both the Magistrates' Clerk's office staff and the post office counter staff had known Mrs Harvey for many years, and frequently asked after Mrs Knight's health.

Neither the authority to collect the money due from the court order for maintenance nor that to collect the pension could be found, but the staff in both places stated that such an authority must have been handed to them originally, otherwise the money would not have been paid – and this money would have amounted to quite a tidy sum over twenty years.

On 9 June 1960 Mrs Sarah Jane Harvey was arrested and charged with the murder of Mrs Knight. She was still in hospital, and the police arrested her in her hospital bed at 6 a.m. At first she feigned astonishment and pretended to be as surprised as her son had been at finding a skeleton in the cupboard – or more accurately a mummy. But she was quick-witted enough to realize that she would have to come up with a good story. She could hardly pretend that she did not know the crippled little old lady who had lodged at her home, and admitted that she had been drawing on her behalf the £2 weekly maintenance her husband had been paying her through the court, and later also the weekly old-age pension. She averred that she had been posting the money to Mrs Knight, who now lived at an address in Pen-y-maes, near Llandudno. The police went to the address, where they were not surprised to find that the occupiers had never even heard of Mrs Knight.

Eventually Mrs Harvey realized that she was trapped in the web of her own lies, and would have to concoct a more plausible explanation for the police. She was not to know that the police did not believe her, but she told them with a wealth of realistic detail that Mrs Knight was very frail and could barely walk owing to her illness. She had been lodging in the house only a few weeks, Mrs Harvey continued, when she heard a noise and found that Mrs Knight had fallen out of bed. 'I am in such pain,' she had said, 'that I would rather be dead.' It seems that Mrs Harvey had taken her at her word ...

Mrs Harvey's statement continued:

> I tried to lift her from the floor to put her back in bed, but she was too heavy. I thought if I went downstairs and made myself a cup of tea I might feel a bit stronger and manage it. When I looked at her I saw she was dead. I was scared stiff, I can tell you. I panicked ... I pulled her along the landing and put her in the empty cupboard before anyone else in the house should come along and see what all the noise was about. I threw her dressing-gown in on top of her.'

For a woman in a panic, the police thought, Mrs Harvey had acted with remarkable aplomb. Before finally locking the cupboard which was to become a mummy's tomb Mrs Harvey hung flypapers in the confined space, and threw a blanket on top of the dressing-gown. Then she continued her life normally as if nothing had happened, taking in other lodgers, including a replacement for the erstwhile occupant of Room No. 2. Her weekly collecting of the deceased woman's money was clear profit, for she no longer had to provide linen, laundry or board. True, she did not receive the weekly rent of thirty shillings, but the amount she drew was more than this.

All these points were aired at length in court at Mrs Harvey's trial, which opened on 30 June in the courtroom at Rhyl Town Hall. The defence based their case on the statement of the accused that she had found her lodger dead – in other words, that she had died from natural causes. The defence averred that it made sense that a woman should panic at finding her lodger lying unexpectedly dead after falling out of bed. But, countered the prosecution, it made no sense at all that the woman's immediate reaction should be to conceal the body. They reasoned that the normal reaction of such a person in these circumstances would have been to try to summon assistance. By inference, such an abnormal reaction must have signified that the death was not accidental at all, but that she had been killed – strangled with a stocking, according to the pathologists with their evidence of a neck groove, the depression on the neck where the knot had been tightened, and depressions in the thyroid cartilages.

The trial, presided over by Mr Justice Davies, dragged on for five days, much of which was taken up by arguments between the various textile experts called by both sides to determine just how much a lisle stocking was capable of stretching when used as a ligature to strangle a person. The passage of twenty years had not made this contentious issue any easier – rather the reverse. In the end, as the judge was at pains to point out, the prosecution was in no position to be able to prove the vital point of whether the stocking had been stretched. 'There seem to be manifold circumstances of suspicion,' he said, 'but when one considers the evidence, it comes to this ... If it cannot be proved that the stocking stretched, then the prosecution fails.'

The accused was an elderly, sick woman, and the crime with which she had been charged occurred twenty years previously. It seemed, therefore, an act of compassion when the judge stopped the trial. 'An act of murder,' he said, 'could not even be unquestionably proved.' Mrs Harvey was therefore found guilty only of the two lesser charges of fraudulently obtaining money from the court and from the post office, and sentenced to a token fifteen months' imprisonment on each charge, the two sentences to run concurrently. In all, Sarah Jane Harvey had received more than £2,000 from her dead lodger, and whether she had strangled her or whether the unfortunate lady had died from natural causes, Mrs Harvey, perhaps, considered her comparatively short term of imprisonment well worth it.

The puzzle still remains unsolved: if Mrs Knight had

indeed died from natural causes, why would there have been the mark of a ligature on her neck – not to mention the remains of a stocking?

9

The Widow of Windy Nook

Mary Elizabeth Wilson (1958)

Windy Nook is a drab, working-class district of Felling-on-Tyne, in the industrial north-east. The widow who forms the subject of our story was equally drab: thick-set, with hair scraped back into a bun, given to wearing heavy, shapeless woollen garments and the heavy black lace-up shoes known to Geordies as 'clodhoppers'. If clogs had been in fashion, no doubt she would have worn them. An ordinary north-country working-class housewife, fond of standing in her overall on the front doorstep with her arms folded and her tongue ready to wag with those of her neighbours – at least that was how her neighbours saw her. But the reality was very different.

Mary Elizabeth Wilson was born in 1892 and, according to the custom of her class in those days, as soon as she was fourteen she left school and was sent out into service.

By the time she was twenty-two Mary Elizabeth (usually known as just Mary) was working in the home of a wealthy builder, whose eldest son was an apprentice – more or less a labourer. Mary was very taken with this young fellow, John Knowles by name, and he, being smitten himself (no doubt Mary was much more attractive in her youth), decided to marry her.

John Knowles was called up in 1914 and, as often happens when newlyweds are separated by war, they grew apart. They did not separate, but the outward shell of their marriage, undertaken with such high hopes, concealed a growing resentment and rancour. They became almost strangers in the same house, barely on speaking terms. For some unknown reason the couple agreed not to divorce, but stayed under the same roof.

Over the years the marriage grew increasingly empty of all meaning. The couple slept in separate rooms, and almost the only time they saw each other was at meal-times – Mary continued to cook for her husband. She eventually took in a lodger, who was a chimney sweep named John George Russell of similar age to her husband. As she was heard to tell a neighbour, 'I might as well cook for three as two – it makes no odds.' But Mary's cooking was not all that the chimney sweep was interested in; a few months after he had come to live in the little terraced house in Windy Nook, she had left her bed and moved into his. Her husband, from all accounts, was fully aware of the situation, and seemed to accept this *ménage à trois* with equanimity. All he wanted was to have good substantial meals served on time, the house kept clean, his linen washed and ironed, and no women's chatter. It was, he opined, a small price to pay. He gave her the weekly housekeeping as usual and the lodger's rent augmented her income.

Eventually the mortgage on the house was paid off and Mary began to feel restless. Perhaps the whole situation had built up until it was just too much for her: the indifference of her husband and, with advancing age, the waning of her lover's affections. He, however, felt he was on to a good thing, and made no effort to move but settled into a comfortable routine which Mary began now to find irksome. The two Johns in her life, she felt, were a dead loss. It was time to do something to change the too-familiar pattern.

In 1955 John Knowles became sick and had to take to his bed. Knowles had always been strong and healthy – he had to be for his job 'on the building' – and had never had a day's illness in his life, not even the usual childhood complaints such as measles or chicken-pox. After a week of his complaining of stomach pains and vomiting, Mary called in a doctor, who prescribed medicine in liquid form; Mary was instructed as to how and when it was to be administered. Mary told a woman friend that 'the medicine didn't seem to be doing him much good.' Five days later he was dead.

The funeral, in August 1955, took place in the normal way, and friends and neighbours who had attended the service and met afterwards at the widow's home noted that she seemed to be very withdrawn and silent, as though overwhelmed by her feelings of grief. Soon afterwards, however, the widow was telling them that 'she felt she needed a change' and started to look round for another house. With the help of estate agents she quickly found a more modern and larger house, still in the Windy Nook district and in fact only a few hundred yards from her present abode. The legal transactions of sale and purchase were carried out, and a few weeks after her husband's death Mary moved to her new home. The chimney sweep went with her.

If she thought that John Russell would marry her, she was mistaken. All he was interested in was a comfortable bed and board with no onerous obligations. Five months after John Knowles had died, the lodger, who had cheerfully agreed to pay a higher rent in his new home, suddenly complained of feeling sick and having no appetite. It was shortly before Christmas 1955. 'This isn't like me,' he told Mary. 'I'm feeling really ill. Ask the doctor to come and see me.' He took to his bed, and the doctor was duly summoned. As in the case of John Knowles, the doctor's nostrums seemed to do the patient little if any good. The unfortunate man's pain increased and he gradually became weaker in body, with trembling limbs. That year's winter was bitterly cold, and Mary made hot milk and hot soup to – as she put it – 'tempt John's appetite and warm him up.'

John's appetite was not tempted, nor was he 'warmed up' – instead, he grew rapidly worse from day to day. The doctor was called in again. 'He's in a bad way,' he said. 'He's not responding to treatment at all, and I'm beginning to fear the worst.' The doctor was right; in late January, John Russell died. The sum of £46 was the total he left Mary.

The good folk of Windy Nook may, perhaps, have

considered it rather odd that two men living in the same household should have died in such quick succession, but it was thought to be just coincidence. Both were 'getting on', as they say – of an age when any severe illness can prove fatal. A doctor had certified that both men had died from natural causes. The supposed coincidence was talked about as a nine days' wonder, and was then forgotten.

Mary Wilson was a very fast worker, and her erstwhile lover was scarcely cold in his coffin when she set about looking for a husband. She was, of course, looking for a man who had money. Eventually her choice lighted upon one Oliver James Leonard, a retired estate agent aged seventy-five. This man lodged with a Mr and Mrs Connolly in Hebburn-on-Tyne, and despite her unprepossessing appearance she seemed to exert some fatal attraction, both literally and metaphorically, for this man, who promptly left his lodgings at the Connollys' home and moved to Windy Nook. But it seemed that things were not going as smoothly as Mary would have liked, for just three days later she and her new lodger had an almighty row. She went to Hebburn-on-Tyne and knocked at the Connollys' door, demanding that the couple come and remove him. 'Get the old bugger out of my house!' she stormed. Mrs Connolly asked her what the trouble was, 'He will not sign any money over to me until he puts a ring on my finger,' she said. 'So come and get the old bugger out!'

It seems that the quarrel did not last long. Mary realized, perhaps, that although her choice had been a little too hasty, an early marriage would be the quickest way of prising any money out of this grasping, miserly old man. It would certainly be the only way. Quite soon after the nuptials had been celebrated at Jarrow Registry Office in September 1956, Oliver Leonard caught severe flu and became unsteady on his legs. Thirteen days after the wedding he was dead.

The drama took place this time in the presence of a neighbour rather than the doctor. On the thirteenth day after the marriage, the neighbour, Mrs Ellen Russell (no relation to the chimney sweep) was awakened at one o'clock in the morning by a frenzied knocking at the front door. Hastily flinging on her dressing-gown and slippers, she opened the door to find Mary in an agitated state, almost incoherent. 'Come quickly!' she cried. 'It's my old man! He's dying!'

Mrs Russell stopped only to put on some outdoor shoes, and rushed around to Mary's house with the distraught woman. Upstairs they found Oliver Leonard lying on the bedroom floor, breathing stertorously, deathly white and in obvious agony, unable to speak. That universal panacea the cup of tea was made, and when offered to the stricken man by Mrs Russell, he knocked it out of her hand. The prosecution was to claim later, at Mary Wilson's trial, that it was clear proof that Oliver Leonard knew that the tea contained poison …

Mrs Russell voiced her thoughts: 'I think he's dying,' to which Mary replied, 'I think so, too. I called you because you will be handy if he does.' Presumably, she had in mind that the woman would be 'handy' for laying him out. This time she did not call the doctor: 'What was the point?' she was later to say. 'Anybody could see that he was going to die anyway.' He did – that same night.

What Mary did was to go round to the doctor's the next day and tell him that her husband had died in the night. He remembered the old man who had called to see him several days earlier and asked for a bottle of cough mixture. The doctor thought that the old man was senile – 'very doddery', as he put it. He concluded that death had followed a severe case of flu combined with old age – he was seventy-five – and did not consider it necessary to go and look at the body. He issued a death certificate to the effect that Oliver had died from myocardial degeneration. The widow collected £50 under the terms of a small life policy the deceased had held.

An unexpected complication was the appearance one morning of James Leonard, the dead man's son by his first marriage, demanding to see a copy of his late father's will. Mary gave him short shrift – not even asking him in for a cup of tea – and told him to go and see her solicitor.

Mary put on a heartrending pretence of grief, and attracted a good deal of sympathy among the locals, most of whom had never heard of the deaths which had occurred at the widow's previous home a few streets distant. 'She has had a lot of bad luck,' said one. 'She deserved better,' averred another. While yet a third was heard to say that it was a terrible tragedy that a woman should be bereaved so soon after the wedding, even if she had married such an old man.

Shrugging off the condolences, the widow left the registry office, slipping the latest death certificate into her handbag (she must have started quite a good-sized collection by that time) and made her way to the undertaker's, which was just around the corner, with whom she haggled over the price of the cheapest deal coffin. The Widow of Windy Nook was as parsimonious as she was grasping.

Mary was deep in thought during the next few weeks. She had learned a bitter lesson – her carefully prepared schemes to rid herself of unwanted men were out of all proportion to the meagre returns. John Knowles had had nothing to leave her but a few sticks of furniture to sell; John Russell had left just £46, and Oliver Leonard £50 under an insurance policy. She must do better next time! In future she would select a life partner (if that was an appropriate term) with much more care. She would have to take longer, too, and make more discreet enquiries into her prospective spouse's background. It was to be thirteen months before she managed to ensnare her next – and last – choice.

Ernest George Lawrence Wilson was another 75-year-old. He was a retired engineer, with £100 invested in the Co-op, a paid-up insurance policy and, he told her, a nice home – which turned out to be only a somewhat dilapidated council house rented for the princely sum of 6s 6d a week. In October 1957 they were married, and Mary sold her house and furniture and moved into Ernest Wilson's home.

For a scheming murderess, Mary Wilson showed an astonishing lack of intelligence. For a start, she was playing very high stakes for remarkably low dividends, and taking incredible risks into the bargain. Unlike many poisoners, she was much too impatient to curb her greed and allow things to run their natural course, but was obsessed with securing a hasty end-result in the least possible time. Even she must have realized that she was pushing her luck, and that sooner or later someone would start noticing the speed with which she disposed of her husbands – and talk. Gossip was rife in such places as the mean streets of Felling-on-Tyne, where back-to-back houses jostled with industrial plants belching smoke and sulphurous fumes. But the Widow of Windy Nook ignored the warning signs that were staring her in the face – signs which would have deterred a more prudent operator. For her, cupidity went hand in hand with stupidity.

The period of grace Mary allowed her latest husband was stretched by a couple of days – to fifteen, to be exact. The usual charade had been gone through – a sudden illness which gradually became worse until death ensued. This time, Mary took the precaution of calling in a different doctor from the one she had employed on the previous occasion. He prescribed medicine in the usual way, and when the patient did not respond – at least to the doctor's treatment – Mary called him in again. When the doctor arrived on this second occasion, to his surprise he found his patient dead. Moreover, he had been dead for several hours – certainly before the doctor had received the call to come to the house. The doctor attributed this delay to the fact that Mrs Wilson was elderly (she was sixty-six) and, as he put it, 'slow in getting around to things' – a description that could hardly apply to some of the things she was fast at getting around to ...

Time was now running out for the much-married widow. Talk had become gossip, and gossip had escalated to rumour – and the rumours had begun to reach people in authority. The behaviour of Mrs Wilson herself had raised a number of eyebrows. For example, when the undertaker came to measure the body of her latest victim for his coffin, she suggested that, since she had put so much business his way, he might quote her a wholesale price! Again, guests who had been invited to the modest wedding reception she had organized to celebrate the marriage remembered how flabbergasted they had been to hear the bride say, when told by the caterer that there would be quite a few leftover cakes, 'Better save them – they will come in handy for the funeral when he pegs out.' Naturally, they thought that it was a joke in very bad taste, referring to the fact that Ernest was seventy-five.

After the funeral, during the customary gathering of friends and relatives at the house afterwards, Mrs Wilson went out in the middle of the afternoon, leaving the guests unattended, saying that she had to get to the shops before they closed. It was discovered that this was in order to sell her late husband's gold watch and chain – just two hours after he had been buried! The unseemly haste which characterized this woman can be compared only to that shown by the odious George Joseph ('Brides in the Bath') Smith.[1]

The doctors who had attended the dead men had no reason to suspect foul play. After all, the average GP was not a forensic pathologist and most – at least in those days – would not have known how to look for signs of poisoning in a dead body. Such things were a matter for the autopsy. And it was difficult to obtain an order for an autopsy unless a physician had reasonable grounds for suspecting that a person had not died from natural causes.

The finger of suspicion that began pointing to Mary Wilson was the result of the tittle-tattle of neighbours. Rumours can grow to mighty proportions, and in time they are bound to reach the knowledge of those whose business it is to ensure that the law is observed. Thus it was that the police of Felling-on-Tyne were made aware of the widow's indiscretions, the haste with which she married, buried and remarried, and the fact that in each case the financial gain on death was larger than the previous one. Not that these gains were large by any standard, but this last case netted the widow more than twice the amount of money she had received last time – £100 plus interest at the Co-op, a matured insurance policy, albeit modest, and the tenancy of the council house. Against this was the fact that Mary Wilson herself had never paid the premium on any policy insuring her husbands' lives, nor had she taken out any new policy for any of them. She appeared to be content with meagre pickings. The police knew that coincidences could happen in real life which could be even more bizarre than some of those depicted in fiction. However, they could not afford to take any chances; while senior officers were trying to make up their minds, this woman could even now be looking for another victim with some savings. The police put two and two together and came up with four: four dead bodies. There had been three legal husbands and one common-law husband, all in the space of two years. Discreet inquiries among the neighbours of the deadly widow only served to reinforce police suspicions. Some of the remarks she had made to her women friends had been incredibly incriminating; for example, on at least three occasions she had been known to ask people who knew the men whether they had any money, how much, and what they intended to do with it. All this before the marriages, of course.

Early in 1958 Mary Wilson was arrested, and a vociferous crowd collected outside the police station, brandishing fists, umbrellas and walking sticks. It must at this point be made clear that she was not arrested merely on the basis of rumour and hearsay; the police had deemed it prudent to obtain an exhumation order for all four of the bodies, and it was the pathologists' findings at the autopsies on these bodies that led directly to the arrest. Detective Inspector Arthur Chapman was the officer in charge of the investigation, in liaison with Dr Ian Barclay, a pathologist from Newcastle-on-Tyne with extensive forensic experience. The local pathologist, Dr William Stewart, carried out the autopsies.

DI Chapman was present, as well as the two pathologists, when the bodies were exhumed, and he put on record a feature which was common to all four. He was struck by the complete absence from the ground around the coffins of insect life of any kind, as well as in the coffins themselves. This in itself was abnormal, and the reason was discovered after the remains had been examined. Phosphorus was found in all four bodies and, as is well known, phosphorus is the main lethal ingredient of Rodine, the rat poison. It kills not only rats but all forms of insect life such as cockroaches, bugs, fleas, beetles and also other invertebrates which inhabit soil, such as worms. No maggots would consume the corpses, for no flies would have alighted on them to lay their eggs.

Dr Stewart found not only phosphorus but also wheatgerm in the organs, which tended to prove that Rodine had been used. This substance contains ground wheatgerm impregnated with yellow phosphorus. In the case of the last two victims, slow decomposition was in its early stages and the phosphorus was easily discernible in lethal quantities, but the first two victims had been buried for twenty-seven and twenty-three months respectively. Yellow phosphorus deteriorates rapidly in a decomposing body; chemically it oxidizes to form a phosphate, and this renders it much more difficult to detect in the tissues. This made the tests much less conclusive, although it could be proved that phosphorus did exist in some parts of the tissues. No evidence could be produced, however, to show how the phosphorus came to be in the bodies, and open verdicts were returned at the inquests on John Knowles and John Russell, which were left on file. Only the charges in respect of the last two victims were proceeded with.

Tests showed that Wilson had had no organic disease despite his advanced age, and that Oliver Leonard's heart was normal although he had some muscular wasting attributable to age. When examining Wilson's body, Dr Stewart found congestion in the oesophagus, stomach and intestines, and the liver was yellow, instead of the normal colour – saturated with phosphorus. Lethal quantities of the poison were found in both bodies. One or two grains of Rodine – about a teaspoonful – is a lethal dose. Changes in the liver were less pronounced in the case of Leonard simply because the body had been buried for a longer period.

The trial, in Newcastle Crown Court, was presided over by Mr Justice Hinchcliffe. The prosecution was led by Mr Geoffrey Veale, QC, while Mrs Wilson was defended by Miss Rose Heilbron, QC. Several different pathologists gave evidence on both sides, including Professor F.E. Camps, Dr David Price and the two doctors who had been present at the autopsies. Conflicting opinions were batted back and forth between them, hinging mainly on the rate of oxidization of phosphorus in a body according to the length of time it has been interred. Much of this technical discussion and argument went right over the heads of the jury of Geordie worthies, whose knowledge of phosphorus was limited to the fact that it was the constituent of Rodine, which left rats very dead.

The method of administration was conjectured. The substance has an unpleasant look and taste, and smells revolting. It leaves a metallic after-taste in the mouth. It could be most effectively diguised, the doctors stated, in cough medicine, jam sandwiches (using a lot of jam), or some other strong-flavoured substance. It was, they averred, highly unlikely that it could be given in tea – the taste and smell would come through.

Professor Camps stated that if Rodine had not been given in tea, the strongest possibility was that it had been put into the cough mixture which both men had been taking in the days before they died. The symptoms of phosphorus poisoning were then described: intense thirst, agonizing stomach pains, vomiting, bowel cramps and prostration. Both men suffered from all these symptoms. The doctors who had attended the two men were asked how it was that they did not diagnose phosphorus poisoning in their patients. One replied that he had seen the patient alive only when he had walked into his surgery asking for cough medicine; the other said he had seen only the dead body. Both said that they had no previous experience of phosphorus poisoning.

Mention was made at this point by the prosecution of the incident in which Mrs Russell, the accused's neighbour, had a cup of tea knocked out of her hand as she tried to give it to Oliver Leonard as he lay on his deathbed. They sought to cite this as proof that Leonard had known that it contained poison. Miss Heilbron, for Mrs Wilson, gave her opinion that it was no such thing. Dying persons, she said, frequently thrash their arms about in agony during their death throes, and Leonard had inadvertently knocked the cup of tea from Mrs Russell's hand. The prosecution pooh-poohed this notion, saying that Miss Heilbron was clutching at straws.

They said precisely the same thing when Miss Heilbron made what they considered to be an extraordinary suggestion to Dr Stewart, a pathologist of vast experience, that because he had examined only sections of the various organs in their entirety, the autopsies he had performed were incomplete. This was indignantly denied by Dr Stewart. It was quite impossible, he said, that the two men could have died naturally when phosphorus was found in their bodies. Miss Heilbron seemed to be on a losing wicket.

At the beginning of the trial, Mr Justice Hinchcliffe refused an application for two separate trials. Owing to the similarity of the two cases, 'system'[2] could be shown, and the judge directed the jury to consider the facts of both cases comparatively. From this, it would eventually become clear that the deaths were neither natural nor accidental, but the result of deliberate poisoning.

Mrs Wilson was not called to give evidence, on the advice of her counsel, who obviously realized that her client was as likely to incriminate herself in the witness-box as she had been in her conversations with her neighbours. When Miss Heilbron revealed that she had given her client this advice, she was rebuked sharply by the judge.

The jury was out for only an hour and a quarter, and brought in a unanimous verdict of guilty of each of the murders. With some show of obvious reluctance, based on Mrs Wilson's age rather than her sex, Mr Justice Hinchcliffe sentenced her to death. However, the Widow of Windy Nook did not hang, for five days after the trial news was brought to her in her cell in Holloway Prison that the Home Secretary had commuted her sentence to life imprisonment. At least she would never again be free to seek out another gullible old man to murder for what little money he possessed.

Four years later she died in prison – from natural causes – aged seventy.

Notes

1. Georgina Lloyd, *The Evil That Men Do* (Robert Hale, 1989).
2. For an explanation of 'system', see the trial of George Joseph Smith in *The Evil That Men Do*.

10

The Butcher's Boy

Gerard Toal (1928)

As we have seen in the last chapter, some murderers are content to kill for very small returns. Incredibly, a few killers are prepared to destroy their victims for pennies. Such a murderer was Gerard Toal, who killed in order to steal bicycle parts which he sold to bicycle-repair shops. The total amount of his ill-gotten gains could not have come to much more than two pounds, if that.

Gerard Toal had recently lost his job at the butcher's (the record does not say why) and had obtained a new position as handyman-cum-servant and chauffeur to the parish priest in the small village of Faughart, near Dundalk, Co. Louth, in Ireland. He was barely eighteen when Father James McKeown, a reserved but kindly man in his middle fifties, took him into his household. He already had a housekeeper, Mary Callan, a 36-year-old spinster, who attended to the cooking, cleaning, laundry and similar duties. Toal's parents had died and he had no family home, so the priest gave him a room of his own above the stables, where Father McKeown kept not only a pony and trap but also an old black Ford car.

On Monday, 16 May 1927, the priest had to go to Dublin on church business, and told Toal to get the car ready to drive him to the station at Dundalk to catch the midday train. As it drew in to the platform, the priest told the boy to take the car home, and then meet him again with the car at 7.40 p.m., when the train would be due in at Dundalk from Dublin, to drive him home.

As arranged, Toal was there punctually at Dundalk

station with the car as Father McKeown arrived on the 7.40 train. As they approached the priest's house they saw a neighbour, a Mrs McGuinness, coming towards them along the road from the direction of the house.

'I wonder what she wants?' observed the priest.

'Oh, I expect she's been to see if Mary is back yet,' replied the youth. An odd sort of remark to make, mused the priest, since the boy had not volunteered the information that Mary had gone out; after all, even if she had, she would have been back long since to prepare their supper.

As the two entered the house, it was obvious that Mary Callan was not there. The table had not been laid in the dining-room, and no preparations were in evidence in the kitchen. Mary's bicycle was also missing from its usual place under the porch by the back door. Curiously, the priest noticed, there was what appeared to be a freshly washed and scrubbed patch on the kitchen floor. The kitchen range fire had been allowed to go out, and there was no hot water for tea or heat for cooking. Father McKeown decided that at this late hour it was hardly worth while getting the fire going again, and said that they would go without supper. The youth made no objection.

While Toal was putting the car away Father McKeown looked into the other rooms of the house, but there was no sign of the housekeeper, nor any note to explain her absence. The priest, finding her room unlocked, opened the door and glanced cursorily round the room, but found nothing amiss, except to note that her best hat and coat were missing from the closet. Closing the door again, he thought it very odd that there should not even have been a message. The only possible explanation, he considered, was that Mary's mother had been taken ill suddenly and she had gone to see her; but, he reflected, it was a long way for Mary to go by bike – the village where her mother lived was a good thirty miles away. Still, she should be back in the morning – no doubt someone she knew in her home village would be giving her a lift. Comforting himself with these ruminations, Father McKeown prepared to turn in for the night as he had to be up early the next day for morning Mass. The boy, never a great talker, was even more silent than usual as he went off to lock up for the night.

When morning came and there was still no sign of the housekeeper, Father McKeown, on returning from Mass, told Toal to light the fire, prepare breakfast, and see that hot water was available – enough of washing in cold water at 6 a.m.! He then asked the boy what one would have expected him to ask him the previous day: what did he know about Mary's disappearance, if anything? Toal – who, one would have thought, would have acquainted his employer with any unusual movements on the part of the housekeeper long before this – stated that after he had returned to the house early in the afternoon and put away the car, he had met Mary, dressed in her best hat and coat and wheeling her bicycle, as he was coming across the yard from the stables, and that she had told him that 'she was going away for good'. She had not said any more, nor had Toal asked her any questions – surely a very strange way to behave, as both of them would have known that her sudden departure would mean serious inconvenience for her employer.

Father McKeown was not a suspicious man by nature, but by now even his credulity was stretched to the limit. First of all, why had the boy not told him this yesterday? Secondly, if she really had 'gone away for good', why would she not take her suitcase and extra clothes, at least? When he had looked round her room, her suitcase was still there, only her best coat and hat were missing, and her books, her Bible, her rosary, family photographs and other possessions were still on her dressing-table and shelves. Very odd … But, as we have seen, Father McKeown was not by nature a suspicious man, and he still felt sure that there must be some reasonable explanation. Yet he could not understand why the boy had waited to be asked, more than twelve hours later, whether he knew anything of the housekeeper's movements and, in particular, why he had allowed him to think, on their return from Dundalk, that she had merely gone out.

The priest then instructed Toal to take the car and go to

Mary's mother's home, to see whether he could find out one way or another what had happened. Mary was not the kind of woman who would just, as we say these days, 'drop out' without at least confiding in her mother. She was a devout Catholic, had no known men friends, and had been in the priest's service for a considerable time, so her employer could be said to have a good knowledge of her character. There had been no problems in the course of her employment; she was sober and industrious and, in the parlance of those days, 'knew her place'.

Toal returned during the afternoon, saying that Mary's mother knew nothing whatever of her daughter's whereabouts, that she herself was perfectly well, and that her daughter had not been to see her at all since her last leave. Toal then added the cryptic comment that 'Mary had something wrong with her, and that is why she went away.' Father McKeown did not pursue the matter or ask the boy what he meant, and Toal seemed anxious to change the subject.

On the following day the priest went to the nearest Garda (police) station, which was located at Síochána, a neighbouring village. He informed the Gardaí that his housekeeper had mysteriously disappeared, taking no belongings except her bicycle, and leaving no note to explain her absence. The Gardaí showed little interest and voiced the opinion that surely it was a little premature to suspect the worst if an employee was absent without notice for a mere two days. She was, after all, a grown woman, not a young teenage girl. On 21 May – four days after Mary's disappearance – Father McKeown went back to the Gardaí at Síochána and told them that it was quite out of character for his housekeeper to stay away for four days without a word, and that he feared something amiss had befallen her.

The Gardaí still shrugged off the priest's enquiries, so on 30 May he went to the larger Garda station at Dundalk which, he considered, might be expected to take a more serious view of the matter than a small sleepy village Garda station would do. This proved to be the case, and two officers were despatched to Faughart to interview the priest, Toal, and a Miss Peggy Gallagher, a friend of the missing woman, who had volunteered to act as housekeeper in her absence. Miss Gallagher knew nothing more about her friend's whereabouts than Toal professed to do – Mary had obviously not confided in her before leaving.

As the two officers left they stated that a superintendent from Dundalk would call to see them the next day. That night Toal was noticed burning things in the grate in his room and also in the open, which he said were unwanted papers, after he had been having a clear-out. He made no secret of these fires, even borrowing matches from Miss Gallagher. The superintendent's expected visit did not, however, materialize.

A week passed. No letter or message of any kind was received from Mary Callan. Her wages were due, but she did not apply to receive them. Nobody had seen her since 17 May, and the Gardaí appeared to be doing nothing. Of course there was plenty of local gossip and speculation as to where she could have gone, but nothing which would help the investigation. Father McKeown became more and more uneasy as time went by and Mary Callan's silence continued. In the summer he went away for two months on a church-sponsored course, and when he returned in the autumn the situation was unchanged. No one knew anything, and he was as mystified as ever.

Toal always kept his room locked, but one day, Father McKeown, seeing it unlocked – a very unusual occurrence – went in on an impulse to look around. He had never been in the boy's room before. In the loft space above the bed he saw a blanket which he knew did not belong to the boy's room. He showed this to Peggy Gallagher, who said it was one of Mary's blankets. When Toal was asked to explain what one of Mary's blankets was doing in his loft, he insisted that it was one of his and not one of hers, and that he kept it in the loft during the summer and early autumn, until he should need it when the colder weather set in. The priest pointed out that it was already November and the weather had grown appreciably colder recently ...

Father McKeown may have been satisfied with this explanation, but Peggy Gallagher was not; and she now decided to make a few investigations on her own account. As her suspicions grew, she finally persuaded Father McKeown to look more closely at Gerard Toal's room, and on 28 March 1928, having kept a lookout for an unguarded moment when the door was left unlocked, he searched the boy's room. This time he found hidden a wheel, front fork, mudguard, saddle and dress-guard from a lady's bicycle, in almost new condition, which had the appearance of having been recently cleaned and polished. In a box he also found a lady's watch, similarly dismantled, which Miss Gallagher said she was sure had belonged to Mary Callan.

When Toal came in to supper that evening Father McKeown did not ask him about the watch, as he knew that the boy liked to try to repair broken watches, and had even repaired his own watch for him on one occasion, as well as watches and clocks for various villagers. But he did question him about the bicycle parts. Toal stated that he had bought various old parts in order to assemble a bicycle to sell, failing which he could sell the spare parts to repair shops. 'I don't believe you,' replied the priest. 'For a start, they are not old parts – they are almost new; and for another thing, they look very much to me like parts from Mary Callan's bicycle.'

Toal indignantly denied that they were parts from Mary's bike, and vehemently insisted that he knew anything at all about her disappearance. He persisted in his story that he had purchased the spare parts from various people in order to assemble a new machine to sell. On the priest's asking him to give as proof the name of any one of these people, Toal said that he had bought the mudguard from a man named Thomas Halfpenny who lived in Blackrock, a village about ten miles away. The priest then told Toal to get the car and drive him to Halfpenny's house to confirm his story. Father McKeown went inside, leaving Toal in the car outside the house, and the priest learned from Thomas Halfpenny's mother that her son had emigrated to America thirteen months previously.

A grim-faced Father McKeown returned to the car. 'You

have told me a barefaced lie,' he said. 'I don't believe a word of your stories about buying the parts. I am going to drive you to the Garda station at Dundalk. You can tell *them* your fanciful stories.' And, so saying, he turned the car about in the direction of Dundalk.

On the way, they drove in silence for some minutes, until the boy suddenly spoke. 'Father,' he said, 'I will tell you the truth. I broke into Williamson's [a bicycle-shop in Dundalk] and stole the parts. I'm sorry ...'

The priest did not slacken speed but continued towards Dundalk. 'So you're a thief as well as a liar,' he told his passenger. 'We will soon know if you're telling the truth this time. The Gardaí will have a report of the burglary.'

At the Garda station it was ascertained from the records that there had never been any break-in at Williamson's and that no bicycle parts had ever been stolen. A sergeant was sent to ask the manager to check his stock, just to make sure, and the manager confirmed that all his stocks of parts were intact. Gerard Toal then again changed his story, stating that a self-confessed thief had given him the parts to get rid of them as he had stolen them and was now in a state of panic as someone suspected him, and begging him not to disclose his name to anyone.

Father McKeown told him that it was no longer possible to know if any word the youth spoke were the truth or not, and he voiced his private suspicions about the missing housekeeper to a senior officer. The Garda replied that a suspected murder with no body and no proof was hardly a basis for keeping Toal in custody, and discharged him home, but said that he would send two officers to search his room, just for the record – perhaps to allay any suspicions Father McKeown might still have lingering in his mind.

The two Gardaí, on searching the room, found more bicycle parts, but the box with the watch parts was missing. Asked where it was, Toal produced it from his jacket pocket, where he had secreted it while the officers' backs were turned. He stated that he had purchased the watch, which would not go, for sixpence from a man he did not know, so that he could try to repair and sell it.

The fireplace was still full of hot ashes, and the Gardaí recovered pieces of a material like sacking or hessian, and the partly burned remains of various items of clothing. Incredibly, the Gardaí left the house, leaving Toal behind to sleep in his room as usual; nor did they attempt to contact either Toal or Father McKeown further.

The whole affair was beginning to tell on the priest's nerves: he had had enough. He gave Toal a fortnight's notice, and the youth said that he would emigrate to Canada. On 7 April 1928 Toal left for Belfast, Father McKeown himself driving him to the station and seeing him on to the train, not without heaving a sigh of relief ...

Driving back to Faughart, the priest wondered whether he had perhaps done the boy an injustice in suspecting him. In all these past eleven months, what proof did he have? The fellow was certainly an inveterate liar, and probably even a thief, but that did not make him a murderer. The bicycle parts might well have been stolen; Mary Callan might well have given him her watch to repair. If Peggy Gallagher was right about the blanket, he might conceivably have borrowed it – or Mary herself might have asked him to look after it when she was not using it, because her room was much smaller than his and she had little space for storage; her room was in the house and had no loft-space, as did the rooms over the stables. As for the Gardaí – if they had thought he might have murdered the missing woman they would have arrested him on some pretext or another; but no, they let him go. And now he was off to Canada without let or hindrance. Perhaps the priest would have more peace of mind now as he returned to his duties. He would have to drive his own car, but that was no great problem ...

Two days later, to everyone's astonishment, Gerard Toal was back in Dundalk. He had stayed with a relative in Belfast while waiting for the next ship to Canada, but was suspected of having broken into a clothier's store in Dundalk before he had left the area and when arrested he had some of the stolen clothes in his possession, and was in fact wearing a stolen suit. He was brought back to Dundalk on this charge, and during the course of interrogation he was again questioned about Mary Callan. A Superintendent Hunt from Dublin Garda headquarters came to Dundalk and questioned him about the bicycle parts which were still ringed round with query marks in their records.

Toal now changed his story once again, this time going back to his previous story of the supposed break-in at Williamson's, which he described in detail. Superintendent Hunt was, of course, certain that Toal was lying, and on 22 May he, with a party of Gardaí, went to Father McKeown's house and searched the gardens. In an ash-pit and under a refuse heap they found part of the bottom bracket of a lady's bicycle, part of the frame of a lady's handbag, a pair of men's trousers from which the left leg and the lower end of the right leg had been torn off, and a rusty and stained penknife in the pocket of the trousers. Near one of the boundary fences they commenced digging operations, and soon unearthed three pieces of a lady's coat, including a distinctive buckle, parts of a woman's jumper and other female clothing, and part of a blanket.

Toal was shown all these things, and stated that he did not know what they were and that he had never seen any of them before. Hunt noticed that the suspect would not look him straight in the face when answering his questions. He was convinced that Toal knew a great deal more than he was admitting. But the discoveries in the garden did not amount to proof of murder. Hunt now decided to search and evaluate the immediate environment of the priest's house.

The house stood near a road junction, beyond which was a small bridge which led into a wood. Through this wood ran a steeply rising path, which the superintendent followed, finally emerging at its summit from the shelter of the trees to a fenced-off area; there, forty feet below, lay the waters of Falmore Quarry. The place was not 500 yards from the priest's house.

The quarry, 390 feet long and 100 feet wide at its widest point, is 45 feet deep in the middle. The banks are sheer except at the spot where Hunt was standing. The quarry is completely surrounded by woods, giving it a dark and forbidding aspect even on a sunny day. Hunt was convinced that here lay the solution to the mystery of the missing woman, and that those dark waters held the grim secret.

The superintendent walked quickly back to the village and telephoned Dublin headquarters, asking them to authorize the Fire Brigade to drain the quarry. Within a few hours the Dublin Fire Brigade arrived and began their mammoth task. After four days' continuous work more than four million gallons of water had been pumped out, and it was on the fourth day, late in the afternoon, as the water level was now falling even more rapidly towards the muddy bottom, that Fire Officer Michael O'Connor observed an object a few inches below the surface, some distance out in the quarry. As the water level fell a little more, O'Connor could see that it was some kind of sack or large hessian bag. The object was retrieved with a shovel and brought to the bank.

Hunt cut open the sack and saw that it contained the remains of a woman's naked body, very extensively decomposed from long immersion in the water. The head and legs had been severed from the body.

Two forensic pathologists, Dr Duggan and Dr Kelly, were agreed that, owing to the advanced stage of decomposition of the body, the exact cause of death was uncertain. There was no evidence of any heart disease or other organic disease, or of pregnancy; the hyoid bone appeared to have been fractured, but this of itself was not sufficient to prove strangulation, although it could possibly have been fractured by manual pressure on the neck. The manner in which the head and the legs had been severed – presumably in order to be able to cram them into the bag with the torso – suggested that the killer had such anatomical knowledge and skill as would be possessed by a butcher to enable him to disjoint a carcase.

Clothing in the sack was proved to have belonged to the missing woman, and a dentist and his assistant both identified false teeth in the mouth of the cadaver as Mary Callan's. The sack had been fastened with a strip of cloth which proved to have been the sleeve of a shirt worn by Toal.

On 4 June 1928 Gerard Toal was charged with the murder of Mary Callan, cautioned, and invited to make a statement. Toal said nothing. And outside the Garda station, a mind-weary Irish priest sat in his car and wept.

* * *

The trial of Gerard Toal took place on 23 July 1928 before Mr Justice Hanna, and lasted four days. Mr William Carrigan, KC, and Mr Dudley White, KC, prosecuted; the accused was defended by Mr Patrick Roe.

Mr Carrigan opened with a vigorous attack on Father McKeown, whom he described as 'one of nature's innocents' and 'a credulous man who had searched everywhere except the one place where there was a veritable mine of information – Toal's room. You would think,' he continued relentlessly, 'that the powers of darkness had darkened Father McKeown's understanding.' Later in the trial, when it came out that Father McKeown had made no fewer than five visits to the Gardaí which evoked no appreciable result, Mr Carrigan made a somewhat half-hearted apology to the unhappy priest for his unwarranted attack.

The next witness was the butcher who had employed Toal as a junior assistant some years previously, but it was never made clear why the accused had left his job. He did, however, give evidence that the accused was skilful in dismembering animal carcases.

A significant piece of evident was that given by a bank manager, who confirmed that the dead woman's savings of £120 were lying unclaimed in the bank. A woman would not have left her savings behind if she were leaving the district, and £120 was a tidy sum in 1928.

Peggy Gallagher was the next witness. Unknown to Toal, she had twice searched his room, and there found Mary Callan's comb, scissors, the watch which she recognized, and her missal (Catholic prayer-book) in which Toal had erased her name, rather clumsily, and written in his own. She also positively identified the bicycle parts as having belonged to the dead woman.

Miss Gallagher also gave evidence of a more dramatic kind. At a gap in the hedge which ran between Father McKeown's garden and an adjoining field, this persistent young lady had found a small piece of sacking, which exactly fitted a hole in the sack fished out of the quarry. This was an achievement for Miss Gallagher, for the Gardaí had missed it altogether. The inference was that the sack containing the body had been carried through the gap in the hedge – or dragged through – and, unknown to the murderer, had caught on, and been torn by, the brambles.

The prosecution's last witness was the manager of Williamson's cycle shop, who was able to confirm that none of his stocks of spare parts was missing, and that Toal's story of a break-in was a complete fabrication.

The defence struggled valiantly to find some loophole of vindication for their client, but were inextricably enmeshed by the tangled web of lies which the accused had woven about himself, 'holding him faster than a spider's web', as one eyewitness at the trial later recorded. The accused was now just nineteen, and was being cross-examined by one of the ablest and most experienced prosecutors at the Irish Bar. Whatever chance, slender thought it be, he might have had of surviving the questioning if he had been truthful, he had no chance at all of extricating himself from the bizarre maze of the lies in which he had lost himself. Recklessly he plunged on unheeding, like a lemming descending to its inevitable destruction, unable to stop. When the judge asked him how he had got into Williamson's, Toal told the most grotesque and palpable lie of all – that he had used one of Father McKeown's house keys which 'just happened' to fit the door, and that he had gone to commit the burglary on the off-chance that this key would fit!

By this time the jury must have found it quite impossible to believe a word that Toal uttered, each one of which was taking him several steps nearer the gallows. He stuck doggedly to his story of the burglary, of buying the watch from a man unknown to him, and of Mary Callan's having told him that 'she was going away for good'. He also denied to the end all knowledge of clothing and other items found buried in the garden or burned in his fireplace, and denied that the shirt sleeve with which the sack had been tied was his, although a witness postively identified it as being the sleeve of a shirt he was seen wearing on the day of the murder.

On the fourth day of the trial, at 9 p.m., the judge finished his summing-up and the jury retired. At 9.37 they came back to ask the judge's advice on a technical point of law, and retired for the second time. Then, only fifteen minutes later, they filed back into the courtroom, with a unanimous verdict of guilty of murder. When the judge asked the prisoner whether he had anything to say or why sentence of death should not be passed upon him, he answered calmly and quietly, 'I am not guilty, my lord.' He then tried to say something else, but failed, the unformed words hanging trembling on his lips. The judge then sentenced him to death as he stood impassive in the dock.

Toal appealed, without success; he then petitioned the government for a reprieve, which also failed. When told he was to die, he seemed totally unconcerned, and never once had he expressed any remorse, or concern over the death of his victim. He was executed on 29 August 1928.

Outside the walls of the prison where he was executed, an ashen-faced Irish priest sat with bowed head in his car. Toal was dead, and had paid for his crime with his life; but for Father McKeown there stretched ahead a whole lifetime of remembering.

11

The Lindbergh Baby Kidnap

Bruno Richard Hauptmann (1936)

Kidnap is an ugly word, and it is never more so than when the victim is an innocent child. And it is most odious of all when that innocent child's life is forfeit for ransom.

Charles Lindbergh is remembered as the first man to have made a solo flight across the Atlantic. On 27 May 1927, when he landed after this daring and prodigious feat, he became the most famous man in the world. But his triumph turned to tragedy five years later, when his nineteen-month-old son Charles Jr. was kidnapped from his cot as he slept.

On 1 March 1932 Charles Lindbergh and his wife Anne were busily preparing for a visit the following day to Anna's parents, who lived in Englewood, New Jersey. The evening passed uneventfully; after Charles Lindbergh had returned home from his New York office, the baby was put to bed at 7.30 by the nurse, Betty Gow, and the cook had supper ready in the dining-room, which was warmed by a blazing log fire. The Lindberghs' home was a large and well-appointed mansion in Hopewell, Hunterdon County, New Jersey – a scant half-hour by car from the New York office.

Just after nine o'clock Charles looked up sharply. 'What is it?' Anne queried as she paused in her packing for the trip.

'I thought I heard a noise,' he said.

'Probably just a crackling log,' his wife rejoined, returning to her task. 'Anyway, time's getting on – I'll ask Betty to go and lock up now.' Since they would be making an early start the next day, they decided to retire earlier than they normally did and by 10 p.m. they had gone upstairs. Not long after this, there was a knock on their bedroom door. It was Betty Gow. 'Mrs Lindbergh,' she said, 'do you have the baby with you?'

'No, of course not,' Anne replied. 'Why do you ask?'

'The baby's gone,' Betty said. 'He's not in his room.'

'Gone? How can he be *gone*?'

'He's not there ...'

'The baby couldn't have climbed out of his cot,' Anne said. 'The bars are far too high, and the safety catch cannot be unlocked from the inside. I'd better come and have a look.' Mr and Mrs Lindbergh had not had sufficient time to prepare for bed, and were still wearing their day clothes. She followed the nurse from the doorway, her husband behind her. Entering the baby's room, they found it undisturbed, but Charles Jr. was not there. The imprint of his head was still on the pillow, and the quilt had been only loosened.

'My God,' Charles Lindbergh said. 'Someone has taken our baby!' Then, spotting a white envelope propped up on the radiator, he went towards it. It had certainly not been there previously.

'Don't touch it!' his wife cautioned. 'Call the police ...'

Betty Gow had scarcely had time to unlock the front door when a car screeched to a halt outside and officers swarmed into the house. A policeman opened the envelope. It contained a ransom demand for 30,000 dollars.

Outside in the garden beneath the window, police found footprints in the mud, well preserved because it had been raining. An officer was detailed to make plaster casts after a makeshift light source had been rigged up from an electric light bulb attached to a lead plugged into the house through a window. By its light the police were able to discern an object nearby, which proved to be a crude home-made ladder, made of three separate sections joined together. There was a split in the wood between the bottom of the top section and the top of the middle one. Such a split would have made a loud cracking noise, and it was this which Lindbergh had probably heard earlier in the evening and which his wife had dismissed as the crackling of a log. No fingerprints were found – it was thought that the kidnapper must have worn gloves. Since his aim had been to remove the child swiftly and without risking disturbing the household by making any further noise, he was unlikely to have taken the time to wipe off any fingerprints from the ladder or any other surfaces he might have touched, such as the window-ledge.

Examination of the ransom note by handwriting experts found that it had been written by a person of German origin who was probably not well educated. There were several spelling errors, such as 'note' for 'not', in the English words used, and in some instances German words had been used: 'gut' for 'good', 'aus' for 'out', and so on. The signature had taken the form of three interlocking circles, but no special significance could be assigned to this. If it had been intended to be cryptic, it had certainly succeeded.

The kidnapping of the famous aviator's son caused a sensation which echoed across America from coast to coast. Only five years previously Lindbergh had been a national hero; now he had been struck by personal tragedy. At this early stage the Lindberghs were confident that their son would eventually be returned to them unharmed as soon as the ransom money was paid. Lindbergh was a rich man, and he was quite prepared to come up with the money, whatever the police decided. His son's life was what mattered.

As the nationwide hunt for the kidnapper moved into action, a Dr John F. Condon, who lived in the Bronx district of New York, sent a letter to his local newspaper offering 1,000 dollars of his own money for the safe return of the child. The doctor was a teacher and lecturer, seventy-two years old, a doctor of philosophy, not a medical man. His letter in the *Bronx Home News* appealed to the kidnapper on the grounds of humanity.

Dr Condon received a reply, forwarded to him from the newspaper, stating that he would be acceptable as a go-between, and signed with the three interlocking circles.

The letter asked Dr Condon to follow the writer's strict instructions, which were to collect the ransom money from Lindbergh and place an advertisement in the *New York American* reading 'Mony is redy' (*sic*), following which Dr Condon would receive further instructions. The notice – with correct spelling – was duly placed in the newspaper, and on 2 April a cab-driver delivered by hand another letter to Dr Condon's house in the Bronx. The instructions, again signed with the triple interlocking circles, told Dr Condon to go out that evening to a florist's shop in the Bronx and to look under a large stone which could be found in front of the building. Under this stone he would find another note telling him where and when to take the ransom money – which the kidnapper had now increased to 70,000 dollars. Because of this, Dr Condon would be allowed a little more time in order to raise the increased amount of money.

The 70,000 dollars ransom money was prepared hastily by Lindbergh at the offices of J.P. Morgan and Company, the bankers, the following day. 50,000 dollars were placed in a wooden box, and the remaining 20,000 dollars wrapped in brown paper-covered bundles. Unknown to Lindbergh, the Treasury had listed the serial number of every bill, issued consecutively in order to facilitate tracing them when they emerged into circulation.

The rendezvous for the handover was the gate to the cemetery in 233rd Street, known as St Raymond's Cemetery. Dr Condon was instructed to walk alone to this place, bringing no one else with him; Lindbergh himself took the doctor to within walking distance of the rendezvous, keeping discreetly in the shadows in the parked car. Lindbergh subsequently stated that he was near enough to be able to hear the kidnapper's voice as he spoke to Dr Condon. He stated that the voice was definitely that of a German who spoke broken English with a heavy guttural accent, and that it was not the voice of an educated man.

Dr Condon had no way of identifying the kidnapper. It was dark, and the man wore a slouch hat pulled down over his face and a scarf tied across the lower half of his countenance. He also wore gloves, so that no identifying rings or other features could be discerned. The man said that his name was 'John' and asked the doctor whether he had brought anyone with him, and also whether he had brought the police. 'No, you can trust me,' Dr Condon replied. The man handed him a note which he said would inform him of the child's whereabouts, and he said that the boy was safe and well and being properly looked after. Dr Condon handed over first the wooden box containing the 50,000 dollars, and it appeared that the kidnapper then panicked, for he ran off into the darkness, leaving the remaining 20,000 dollars of the ransom money behind in the doctor's hands.

The note, signed as usual with the three interlocking circles, stated that Charles Lindbergh Jr. was being held captive on a boat, called the *Nellie*, anchored off Elizabeth Island, near the area known as Martha's Vineyard in Massachusetts. It also stated that the kidnapper would send Lindbergh the baby's pyjamas as a token of good faith by the next morning's mail. The pyjamas were received early the next day, as promised, and the Lindberghs immediately identified them as those the baby had been wearing when he had been abducted. Thus heartened, they immediately set about preparing to go to the location the note had specified and reclaim the boy. Police also joined in the search, keeping a low profile, but it became increasingly clear as the area was gone over with a fine-tooth comb that there was no such boat, and that the boy was not there. The search was nothing if not thorough: police boarded all boats moored anywhere around the island and questioned boat-owners and the proprietors of stores catering for yachtsmen, fishermen and others. No one had seen any man or child who was unfamiliar to them.

*   *   *

On 12 May 1932 a lorry-driver named William Allen was walking in the woods about four miles from the Lindbergh estate with his dog when his attention was drawn to what looked like a shallow grave covered with leaves. On investigating further, he saw that the grave contained the badly decomposed body of a small child. Betty Gow later identified the shirt in which the body was dressed as a shirt she had made out of a flannel petticoat she no longer needed. The autopsy on the body found that the boy had been killed by a blow to the head on the same night as that on which he had been taken from his cot.

The police hunt now switched from the search for the boy to the search for the kidnapper-murderer. First of all efforts were made to trace the wood used to fashion the makeshift ladder which the kidnapper had used to enter the baby's bedroom. It was never established how the abductor had known which window led into the child's room, but it was assumed that he had previously kept watch on the house, hidden outside in the shubbery, until he spotted a child being put to bed through one of the lighted first-floor windows.

Timber experts were called in, and a US Forestry Service scientist was able to identify not only the kind of wood used but the particular timber yard from which it had originated. Arthur Koehler, the scientist in question, took several months to locate the yard, which was on the premises of the National Lumber and Millwork Company in the Bronx. This tended to confirm the police's already strong suspicion that the kidnapper lived somewhere in the Bronx district. This view was further reinforced by the speed with which he had spotted Dr Condon's letter in the *Bronx Home News*.

The police had in the meantime issued a list of the serial numbers of all the currency bills used to make up the ransom money to all banks, large stores, gas and service depots, theatres and cinemas, but it was more than a year before the ransom money started getting into circulation. On 15 September 1934 a customer in a dark-blue Dodge sedan drove into a garage in the Bronx for petrol, tendering a ten-dollar bill. The attendant, who had a copy of the list of serial numbers, checked it against these in his office when he went to get change from the till. Seeing that the money was suspect, he made a quick note of the car's registration number from the office window, the car being parked beside the pumps not far away. He scribbled this note on the ten-dollar bill itself: a New York licence plate, number 4U-13-41.

Police quickly traced the car through the New York State Motor Vehicle License Bureau. The Dodge belonged to one Bruno Richard Hauptmann, a German immigrant, by trade a carpenter, who resided at 1279 East 222nd Street, in the Bronx. The gas attendant had told the police that the man tendering the ten-dollar bill had spoken very poor English with a strong German accent. That same night, police surrounded the small frame house where the suspect lived, waiting throughout the hours of darkness until Hauptmann should emerge. Their patience was rewarded. He left the house and got into his car – the blue Dodge – which was parked outside. They decided to let him drive off and follow him in their own cars, possibly because they considered that a man with both hands on the steering wheel of a car in a busy thoroughfare would be unlikely to pull a gun. A few minutes later, three police cars forced the Dodge over to the kerb. Hauptmann was unarmed.

The police took Hauptmann back to his home, where a search revealed 14,000 dollars of the ransom money, carefully concealed in an outbuilding. Hauptmann, questioned about this money, insisted that it belonged to a friend named Isidor Fisch, a fellow-countryman who had temporarily gone back to Germany, leaving his money in Hauptmann's care. A further twenty-dollar bill with a listed serial number was found in his wallet. He was asked why he was in fact using this money if it belonged to Fisch. Hauptmann replied that Fisch had since died, and that since Fisch owed him 7,500 dollars anyway under a carpentry business partnership agreement they had entered into in 1932, he was entitled to it. Of course the police did not believe his story, and took him into custody pending further and more thorough search of his house.

Forensic experts struck oil when they examined inch by inch the floor of the attic. A piece of the wooden flooring was missing, and sawdust in the area proved that it had been sawn out. Experts matched it to a rung of the ladder which had been found propped against the wall under the nursery window at the Lindbergh home. The original rung had been removed, having probably been broken in some way, and had been replaced by a new rung made from the attic floorboard. When the forensic scientists removed this replacment rung from the ladder and placed it in position in the attic floor, four nail holes in this rung matched exactly four nail holes in the joists below. This was taken as proof that Hauptmann had made the ladder. When he was tackled on this point, he replied scornfully that he was a skilled carpenter and would never have made such a ladder, which was quite obviously the work of an unskilled amateur and not that of a man who took pride in his craftsmanship.

Hauptmann's background was now gone into by police researchers, who discovered that he had entered America illegally in 1923 and soon afterwards married a waitress in order to obtain legal status as an American citizen. The couple no longer lived together but were not divorced and had no children. In Germany, he had been a soldier in the army, and had a criminal record, mostly for burglary. In one of his burglaries he had used a ladder to enter the house, although the record did not state whether the ladder had been made by Hauptmann himself or not.

A further find, on a later search of Hauptmann's home, revealed Dr John Condon's telephone number, scrawled on the inside of the door of a cupboard. Dr Condon was brought to police headquarters and placed in an adjoining room to one in which Hauptmann was taken to answer to questions from a senior officer. Condon was then asked whether the suspect's voice resembled the voice of the man he met at the cemetery gates who called himself 'John' and accepted the ransom money. Dr Condon replied that the voice was identical.

Hauptmann was formally arrested on 19 September 1934, and his trial for the murder of Charles Lindbergh Jr. opened on 2 January 1935 in Flemington, New Jersey, before Judge Trenchard. The Attorney General, David Wilenz, prosecuted, and Hauptmann was defended by

Edward Reilly, who in desperation insinuated that Betty Gow and another female servant in the Lindbergh household were not above suspicion. These preposterous allegations were quickly thrown out as rubbish by the prosecution, who put in an impressive array of witnesses to clinch their case, from the indefatigable Arthur Koehler, the timber scientist, to the alert petrol-pump attendant who had had the presence of mind to jot the number of the blue Dodge on the back of one of the numbered ten-dollar bills.

On 13 February 1935 the court found Bruno Richard Hauptmann guilty of murder. Hauptmann appealed, and after some protracted legal manoeuvring, the appeal was thrown out in October by the Court of Appeals. The prison governor, Harold Hoffmann, visited Hauptmann in the condemned cell, where the prisoner insisted that he was innocent despite all the evidence stacked against him, and demanded that he be given a lie-detector test. His request was refused. Governor Hoffmann's actions were considered by the American Press to be merely a publicity-seeking exercise, while government officials felt that he was politically motivated, since it was common knowledge that he was trying to get the Attorney General ousted from office.

On 3 April 1936 Hauptmann went to the electric chair in Trenton State Prison, New Jersey. He was thirty-six. The remainder of the ransom money – 36,000 dollars – was never found.

12

The Four Pound Killing

Russell Pascoe and Dennis John Whitty (1963)

The story of the victim in this case is a very strange story indeed – so strange, in fact, that it is hardly credible. But truth is stranger than fiction, as events have often proved.

William Garfield Rowe was born in 1899 in Porthleven, a tiny fishing village in Cornwall. Like most teenage youths he was drafted into the Army as soon as he was old enough, in 1917. The army life, however, did not appeal to him and he deserted only a week after joining. When he made his way back to his family home in Porthleven, his parents sympathized with his predicament and, far from urging him to give himself up, gave him £50 – a large sum of money in those days – to help him on his way as he went on the run. They knew that he could not stay at home, because the military police would look for him there first of all.

But catch up with him the military police did, quite soon after he had left Porthleven. However, William Rowe was an ingenious lad with an inventive turn of mind, and devised an unlikely method of effecting his escape. He managed to turn on the mains water supply in the guardroom toilets and washrooms in such a way that the entire ablution block rapidly flooded, and in the confusion, he nipped out when the doors were unlocked to allow in the plumbers. Scaling a fifteen-foot wall, and dropping nimbly to the ground on the other side without injury, he sprinted across the fields and gained the cover of a wood. He was free once more.

He knew that the military police would not think he had

gone home again this time but that he would try escape elsewhere, so young William did precisely what the army authorities thought he would not do – he made for home. This time his parents decided to hide him on their smallholding. He had reached home unseen under cover of darkness, and his parents realized that really they had no other option. Army life was clearly not suited to their son's attitude and psychological make-up, or he would not have deserted in the first place after only seven days, nor made such a daring escape after his recapture.

William became an 'invisible man' holed up in an upstairs room by day, and working at night on the smallholding. Neighbours were told that he had been killed in France in the trenches.

For an incredible thirty years he lived this half-life in the shadows, officially listed as dead. Anyone with more sophistication than he and his family would have realized that if he had given himself up his punishment for his desertion would have been detention in the guardroom until the end of the war and then a dishonorable discharge – surely preferable to thirty years' effective incarceration in a world where he could never go out openly, meet anyone at all except his parents, brothers and sisters, marry and have children, or work anywhere else than on his parents' little farm in a remote corner of Cornwall. His outdoor life was lived in darkness; he could never spend the days in the sun as he toiled, or hear the birds singing in the hedgerows. His parents did him a disservice by hiding him from the normal world.

The Second World War came, and his parents dared not obtain for him the identity card, ration book or clothing coupons to which he was entitled. Somehow they managed to provide him with clothes over this enormous period of time from jumble sales and 'make do and mend'. Food was less of a problem since they grew most of it on their smallholding, kept chickens, pigs and sheep, and a cow for milk.

Eventually William Rowe's father died, and the family moved to a neighbouring village called Constantine, where they found a solidly built, four-bedroomed Cornish farmhouse with a few acres. As the move to the new house was not very far, they took their furniture and possessions by horse and cart. Incredible as it may seem, William Rowe lay hidden under the pile of blankets, quilts and bedspreads.

By 1954, William's elder brother Stanley had died, and another brother had emigrated to Australia. His two sisters were married and lived in other parts of the West Country. William and his mother were left alone to run the farm, named Nanjarrow. His mother worked on the farm by day, while William did his share of the work by night.

When eventually his mother died, he wondered how he would survive. But, fortuitously for him, the newly crowned Queen declared an amnesty for all deserters from both World Wars, and the recluse came out into the open for the first time. He went to the police, declared himself, and was officially reinstated in the land of the living.

After thirty-nine years as a total recluse, William Rowe found it hard to break the habits of half a lifetime. His new-found freedom did not go to his head. He continued to live on the farm, and he managed to keep it going single-handed, after a fashion, but he ventured out only to obtain essentials. He rapidly gained a reputation for keeping himself to himself, and spoke very little to anybody.

Inevitably, the gossips had a field day. Elderly recluses are almost always thought to have fortunes hidden in their houses, and William Rowe's reputation was no exception. In 1960 the farmhouse was burgled, the intruders escaping with about £200 in cash and a quantity of jewellery which had belonged to the old lady. The burglars were never caught. The police could not even locate a possible suspect.

Three years passed, during which time the 64-year-old farmer was seen from time to time in the village purchasing various items from the shops or ordering goods such as horsefeed. When time passed and he was no longer seen on market days or at other regular times, villagers became concerned and wondered whether he might have died. One of them decided to pay Nanjarrow Farm a visit to see if he could find out what had happened to 'the old boy', as the villagers called him. He had last been seen alive at about 9.15 in the evening on 14 August. The following day he would normally have been seen attending a livestock auction, but did not turn up. The visitor to the farm knocked for some time, but could not obtain any response. At about twelve noon he went to see the local police constable and asked him to accompany him back to the farm, as he felt that all was not well.

The officer effected an entry and looked around, the villager who had called him at his heels. They found William Rowe dead near the back door which led to the stockyard. His body was covered in blood, and a trail of blood led from the front door to the spot where his body lay. It seemed evident that he had gone to the door in answer to a knock, and had come face to face with his killer. The house had been ransacked from top to bottom, but the intruder had missed £3,000 which had been well hidden, but which was found by the police who searched the house for clues. It was obvious that this was what the burglar had been looking for.

The constable who had found the body, PC James, and his colleagues who had been detailed to go over the house, reported their findings to their superior officer, who decided to call in the Cornwall County Constabulary and ask them to send their Murder Squad to take over the case. This consisted of Detective Superintendent Thomas Walker, Detective Superintendent Richard Dunn, Detective Inspector Robert Eden and Detective Sergeant Norman Acott. They set up a Murder Incident Room in the local school, but when results were not forthcoming they called in Scotland Yard, who sent Detective Superintendent Maurice Osborn and Detective Sergeant Andrew McPhee to assist.

The medical evidence revealed by the autopsy on William Rowe's body bore witness to the savagery of the frenzied attack which had killed him. He had been stabbed thirteen times: seven times in the head, five times in the chest, and had had his throat cut. In addition, his skull had been shattered and his jaw fractured. One of the chest wounds had penetrated the heart.

Police knew that the burglar who had killed William Rowe had a good head start on them, since the autopsy findings tended to confirm that the time of death was around midnight on 14 August. It was now two days since the murder. Roadblocks had already been set up, but since obvious suspects seemed to be thin on the ground the police resorted to the tactic of stopping every male person who was, or appeared to be, over sixteen, and asking him to come to the murder headquarters to answer routine questions as to his whereabouts on the night in question.

One such male person so stopped was a motorcyclist aged twenty-three named Russell Pascoe, who lived in the village. Asked for an account of his movements, he said that he stayed that night in a caravan owned by his friend Dennis John Whitty, aged twenty-two, and three nineteen-year-old girls. He said he had read of the murder of William Rowe in the local newspaper. When DS Osborn asked him whether he had known Rowe personally – since both lived in the village – he replied, 'Yes, mate. I have known him for yonks. I worked for him three years ago.'

Three years ago ... that struck a chord in the policeman's memory. Only yesterday he had been reading the local police report, in which the 1960 burglary was described ... could it be more than just a coincidence?

It was decided to take Pascoe, Whitty and the three teenage girls in for questioning to Falmouth Police Station. Once there, the girls soon admitted that the two men had asked them for nylon stockings to use as face masks as they were planning to 'do a job' that night. They also warned the girls not to 'blab' to anybody and to say that they had been in the caravan with them the whole night if anyone asked them where they had been.

Local police knew Pascoe and Whitty to be 'hard cases' – always ready to cock a snook at the law. But, faced with six stern-faced senior officers, including two from Scotland Yard, their bravado soon crumpled and their façade of macho demeanour wilted as they realized that there was no way out from the consequences of their crime. It was not long before they admitted that they had left the caravan on the night of the murder armed with an iron bar, a knife and a starting pistol, and had set out on Pascoe's motorcycle intending to commit robbery at the Rowe farm.

The following day Pascoe's girlfriend had showed him the local paper carrying details of the murder, and asked him whether he and Whitty had been involved. 'Yes, we were,' he replied. He went on to tell her that there had been 'some trouble' – by which the girl understood that he meant that the farmer had put up more resistance than he would have expected an old man to do.

On the morning of 17 August Russell Pascoe was charged with the murder of William Rowe. 'I'll tell you the truth,' he replied.

His statement read:

> Last Wednesday night with my mate Dennis Whitty I went to Mr Rowe's farm. We went on my motorbike, and we knocked on his door at about eleven o'clock. The old man came to the door ... I hit him on the back of the head when he turned round with an iron bar. I only meant to knock him out, that's all. He [Whitty] took the bar from me and went for him. Then he went mad. I told him that was enough, but he went for him with the knife. I had to walk away ... I went into the sitting-room and looked round. I found £4 hidden under the piano. Then Dennis came into the room and said, 'The old man's a goner. Let's get out of here.' He took two large boxes of matches, then went back to the old man and took off his watch and took his keys from his pockets. We shared the £4. I have spent my half share.'

The police asked Pascoe why he had not tried to stop Whitty attacking the old man. 'I didn't try to stop him,' he replied, 'because he had the knife and I thought he would stick me if I interfered. I couldn't stop him – he was going mad. I had to walk away. Dennis said he finished him off when he cut his throat. I only knocked him on the head with the bar – I only knocked him out.'

When Whitty was interrogated, and told that his partner

in crime had admitted to his part in the attack on the farmer, Whitty, predictably, tried to shift the blame on to his partner. 'Pascoe made me stick him. I stabbed him in the chest. Pascoe made like he was going to hit me, so I stuck him in the neck.' He buried his head in his hands and started to sob. 'We are both over twenty-one, so I suppose we will hang. I want to tell you about it. I was going to give myself up if you hadn't brought me in.'

Both Pascoe and Whitty made statements blaming each other for the actual killing, and at the magistrates' committal hearing Mr John Woods, on behalf of the Director of Public Prosecutions, told the court: 'The obvious motive for this murder was theft. Never has the well-worn phrase 'a savage and brutal attack' been more typified than in this case.'

The murder trial took place on 29 October 1963 at Bodmin Assizes before Mr Justice Thesiger. The jury of nine men and three women heard both men plead not guilty. For the prosecution Mr Comyn, QC, described the killing as 'one of the most horrible and gruesome murders ever known in this county or, indeed, in this country.' But nevertheless he urged the jury 'not to let horror blind you to the need for care and consideration in reaching your verdict.'

For Whitty, Mr Norman Skelhorn, QC, suggested to the jury that the accused was 'acting under the influence, fear and pressure of Pascoe.' He pointed out how it was Pascoe who had instigated the robbery, and that Pascoe had admitted to the robbery of the victim three years earlier, when he had robbed Mr Rowe of £200. He also quoted from Whitty's statement to the police that Pascoe had threatened him when he tried to demur, saying, 'You will come with me. If you don't, I will scar you for life.'

Speaking in his own defence, Whitty stated that from time to time he suffered from blackouts, which was why he did not own or drive a motorcycle himself although he was interested in bikes. He always rode pillion on his friend's (Pascoe's) machine. Such a medical background, Mr Skelhorn later said, should be taken into consideration by the jury, in order to assess whether this could allow a verdict of guilty of manslaughter by reason of diminished responsibility.

Mr Justice Thesiger told the jury in his summing-up that it was for them to decide whether Whitty acted under fear of injury or death from Pascoe. As to his mental state, the judge continued, the simple fact of law was that a man was adjudged sane if he knew what he was doing and knew that what he was doing was wrong, to the extent that he knew that he would be punished for what he was doing if caught. Finally, he pointed out that no evidence had been forthcoming of any blackout on the night of the murder.

The jury was out for four and half hours, finally arriving at a verdict of guilty of murder against both men. Mr Justice Thesiger donned the black cap, and sentenced them both to hang for their cowardly crime of killing a defenceless old man for the paltry sum of £4, having been led to believe that he kept a fortune in the house.

Both men appealed, and both their appeals were dismissed. The executions were set to take place on Tuesday, 17 December. Russell Pascoe was to be hanged at Bristol, Dennis Whitty at Winchester. A petition for a reprieve was instituted in Falmouth, but attracted only 600 signatures. The two hangings therefore took place as scheduled, both at the same time of 9 a.m.

The lawyers acting for the estate of William Rowe must have made a more thorough search of the farmhouse than the police had done, for they found a diary, written in Esperanto, the international language invented by Dr Zamenhof. Esperanto was one of several languages the farmer had studied to while away the lonely daylight hours when he had to keep to his room during the days of his hiding from the outside world. The diary gave the location of a 'treasure map' which would, when found, in its turn give directions for the finding of the farmer's life savings, which were hidden in the house. Like many eccentric recluses, he had a distrust of banks.

The solicitors acting for his estate followed the instructions on the 'treasure map' and located the money. It amounted to more than £3,000, stuffed into a large glass jar, sealed and covered with grease, and buried under the stone floor of the dairy. In addition, another jar of banknotes was found buried under the concrete floor of a cowshed. In all, nearly £7,000 was found. This is what the two men had been looking for, and the reason why they had come to their ignominious end. But they had settled for only £4 as the price of the old man's life.

13

A Process of Attrition

Dorothy Matajke (1987)

The Kinseys were a devoted married couple who had been together for fifty years. Paul was seventy-two, his wife Opal one year younger. Their life in Little Rock, Arkansas, had seen the usual high spots as well as the more difficult times, but overall it had been a happy one. But in 1985 the friendly, outgoing Mrs Kinsey became ill, and doctors diagnosed cancer. She knew that she did not have as much time left in this life as she would have liked, but accepted it with a quiet resignation.

Her husband was himself elderly and was not fit and energetic enough to care for her himself single-handed, but she had expressed a wish to remain at home with him and not live out her last days in some nursing home. So, in accordance with her wishes, Paul set about looking for a kindly woman who would live in and act as home help, nurse and cook. Her duties would include general housekeeping, paying the bills and purchasing groceries, and seeing that his wife took her prescribed drugs at the proper times.

Paul Kinsey considered himself fortunate that he did not have to wait very long before he found just the person he was looking for. She was 57-year-old Dorothy Matajke, who had moved to Little Rock from Iowa two years previously, and who had advertised in the local paper, offering her services to care for the elderly, the chronic sick and the terminally ill. She could not advertise herself as a nurse, because she had no formal nursing qualifications. She presented Paul with impeccable testimonials from some of her former clients.

Once installed in the Kinsey houeshold, Dorothy Matajke proved very capable, always cheerful and trying to keep up her patient's spirits. Her attitude inspired confidence, and Paul found no cause for complaint. But despite the unremitting care and attention Dorothy lavished on his wife, her condition deteriorated from day to day, and on 5 April 1935 she died, much sooner than her husband had expected. Her death was attributed to terminal cancer. She died only thirteen days after Dorothy had joined the family to take care of them.

During that time, Dorothy had rarely left her patient's bedside, day or night. No one else had given her food or drink or administered her medicine. And now that she was gone, Dorothy turned her energies to caring for Paul with the same devoted attention as she had given to his wife. Paul's own health was frail, but after his wife's death he became profoundly depressed; grief had reduced him to a shadow of his former self. He took to his bed more and more frequently, as if unable to face life as a widower; he seemed to have lost the will to live. In vain Dorothy tried to cheer him up with her affable chatter. She continued to care for him, performing all the household tasks and never intruding on his private sorrow. Paul left all the responsibility of running the home to Dorothy and gave her complete authority.

With only the one client to look after, Dorothy thought that she should look around for a few more. She would be based in Paul Kinsey's house as live-in companion-housekeeper, but would take additional clients on a daily basis. She would answer advertisements for 'home help wanted' in the local paper, and sometimes her clients would recommend her by word of mouth. And thus it was that on 9 September 1986 she acquired another client, a Miss Marion Doyle, aged seventy-four, who was in an advanced stage of terminal cancer.

Ten days after Dorothy had taken Miss Doyle under her wing, the old lady died, on 19 September. But the doctors did not give cancer as the cause of death. They had found an empty bottle beside her body – a bottle which had contained barbiturates. It seemed that Miss Doyle had decided to end her life of pain with an overdose of drugs. So her demise was ascribed to suicide. In accordance with the law, the doctors called in the police, and a sobbing Dorothy Matajke told the officer sent to investigate the suicide that she had left Miss Doyle alone for only a short time while she had to go out to purchase some food. She also informed the officer that Miss Doyle had often told her that she would like to die, to put herself out of her misery; this she construed as a suicidal disposition. What she was unable to tell them, however, was how Miss Doyle could have obtained the bottle of lethal pills. The police duly noted Dorothy's statements.

Dorothy laid out the body and arranged the funeral, and in the meantime continued to look after Paul Kinsey, whose health was now giving rise to some concern. He was refusing food and drink, and even refusing to take his medicine. Members of his family came to visit him and, seeing his condition, decided to have him admitted to hospital. To their surprise, they observed that his housekeeper-companion objected most strongly, vigorously protesting that he did not wish to be moved. They ignored her and took him to hospital anyway. He had hardly been installed in the ward when Dorothy Matajke turned up in the emergency room where he was receiving medical treatment to visit him. But even as she hovered near his bedside Dorothy herself had two visitors – the Little Rock police. She was arrested and charged with forging a number of cheques on Miss Doyle's account.

One of Dorothy's duties which she performed for Miss Doyle had been paying her bills. When Miss Doyle's executors began their audit of her estate, the first discrepancy they noted was a cheque for 1,100 dollars drawn in favour of Dorothy Matajke and which purported to be for the monthly rent of the house for September, but it was found that a cheque for that month's rent had already been drawn previously and paid to the owner of the house. Subsequently, more cheques were discovered, apparently signed by Miss Doyle, for a total of 2,600 dollars, all made out to Dorothy Matajke. The suspect cheques were sent to the Arkansas State Crime Laboratory for forensic examination by handwriting experts, with samples of both Miss Doyle's and Dorothy Matajke's handwriting and their undisputed signatures.

While Dorothy was in custody, the police obtained a search warrant for her rooms at the Kinsey home, where they found several bottles of Librium (a tranquillizer) and three barbiturate drugs. They also found three bottles of an arsenic-based rat poison.

Meanwhile Paul Kinsey, in hospital, was having a number of tests carried out. Before his admission he had become emaciated, his weight having dropped dramatically, and he had been plagued by vomiting and diarrhoea. These two latter symptoms had abated since his admission, and he was being fed protein supplements to try to restore his strength and build him up. The blood and urine tests he now received were to establish what, if any, toxins might be present. The doctors – and the police – were not in the least surprised to find evidence of arsenic in both urine and blood.

A court order was obtained to have Marion Doyle's body exhumed. The exhumation took place on 23 October 1986. The autopsy findings indicated that there was too little of the barbiturate drug in her system to have caused death, so suicide could definitely be ruled out. But enough arsenic was found in her organs to kill fifteen people!

On 24 November Dorothy Matajke was charged with the first-degree murder of Marion Doyle, and also with attempting to murder Paul Kinsey. The death of his wife was attributed to the natural process of attrition, and was not investigated ...

The police now turned their attention to checking Dorothy's background. She had worked as a part-time employee for the Visiting Nurses' Association, an organization which did not require that its employees be qualified nurses who had passed the requisite state examinations. She had been dismissed on 25 September for 'failure to comply with company policy', whatever that might mean; whatever the reasons had been, they did not appear in the Association's records. However, there could have been no connection with the death of Miss Doyle, since the investigators did not contact the Association until 8 October.

It was soon established that the cheerful and affable companion-housekeeper had spent at least fifteen years in the same profession in her home state of Iowa before moving to Little Rock, Arkansas. Detective Mark Seebohm, of the Iowa State Police Department, immediately felt that the name Dorothy Matajke was familiar. Looking up the crime records, he quickly found that Dorothy had worked there as a nurses' aide for the terminally sick and that several persons had died while under her care. Naturally, at least some proportion of these details could be attributed to the normal process of attrition due to age aggravated by cancer and other serious diseases. But in 1973 she had been sentenced to five years in prison after being convicted of fraud charges connected with her patients.

This light-fingered lady managed to get loose in February 1974, when she escaped from the Iowa State Correctional Facility for Women. She remained free for six years, during which time she continued her career of caring for the elderly and terminally ill under various aliases, such as Dorothy Matthews, Doris Mathieson and Dora Meredith. It is conjectured that several of her elderly charges may have become terminally ill after she started caring for them in her own way ...

Dorothy was recaptured in 1980 and served the remainder of her prison sentence, being paroled in 1983. Immediately after her release on parole she moved to Little Rock.

Meantime, what of Paul Kinsey? He was to fight the battle for survival for four months. But systematic doses of arsenic had weakened his system, and on 10 February 1987 he died. Hardly had he been laid to rest when the charge of attempted murder against Dorothy was dropped and a charge of first-degree murder substituted.

The trial was set for June 1987, with a jury of eight men and four women. The charge of murdering Paul Kinsey was to be tried first. The case received nationwide publicity, and the courtroom was jammed with reporters, photographers and spectators, with members of the public who had been unable to obtain a seat milling outside.

Investigating officers testified that they had searched the homes of both victims and found cartons of orange juice, yoghurt, bowls of soup, and non-prescription cough mixture in the fridge, all heavily laced with arsenic. A bottle of 'Terro' ant killer, an arsenic-based preparation, was found in a linen closet in Marion Doyle's home.

A woman relative of Paul Kinsey testified that on one occasion when she visited Paul he was complaining of flu-like aches and pains, nausea and vomiting, and swelling in various parts of the body. The woman further testified that Paul told her that he was 'afraid to take any food or drink that Dorothy had offered him, or take the medicine she gave him, because he was always sick afterwards and he thought Dorothy must be trying to poison him.'

The witness continued her testimony by telling the court that he had told her several times that he did not want Dorothy to stay there and that he would like to get someone else, but he was helplessly bedridden and unable to do anything about it. He had asked Dorothy to leave, but she refused, saying that he would have no one to look after him. The relative discovered on her last visit to his home that Dorothy had drawn two cheques on his account, each for 100 dollars. He had told her that he did not remember signing any cheques. These additional suspect cheques were sent to the forensic laboratory, where they were found to be forgeries, thus adding further evidence to the rapidly growing file.

The coroner, Stefan Nawojczyk, gave evidence of the symptoms and results of arsenical poisoning administered over a protracted period. 'Symptoms include violent vomiting, diarrhoea, influenza-like joint pains and general lethargy,' he said. 'Some victims are treated for flu … Small amounts [of arsenic] given over a period of time can made it look like a natural death. People whose health has deteriorated are more susceptible than healthy individuals.'

The trial lasted for only one day. This brevity could, at least in part, be attributed to the fact that the defence presented no witnesses, not even the defendant herself. A further contributory reason was that the jury took only six minutes to reach a verdict. Dorothy Matajke was found guilty of murder and given a life sentence.

In August her trial for the murder of Marion Doyle took place. Dorothy Matajke entered a negotiated plea to first-degree murder, plus negotiated pleas to five charges of forging Miss Doyle's signature to cheques and two charges of theft of her victim's property. She was sentenced to sixty years in prison for the murder and ten years each on the other seven charges.

While Dorothy Matajke is serving out her sentences in a much more secure prison than the one she previously occupied in Iowa, the Arkansas police are investigating the medical histories of all her patients, living or dead, in that state, and the Iowa police are similarly delving into the medical backgrounds of the elderly and terminally ill men and women she 'cared for' – to use her own term – while she was living there. If suspicious circumstances are revealed, some exhumations may be ordered, and the subsequent autopsies might well reveal that Dorothy had only two great loves in her life – money and arsenic.

14

The 'Legs Diamond' of Worthing

John Victor Terry, Alan Hosier and
Philip Tucker (1961)

John Victor Terry was what is popularly called 'a handful'
even at the tender age of seven. Brought up by an aunt
and uncle, he was resentful that his parents had
abandoned him to the care of relatives, the reason for
which was never made clear. His two pet dogs were
destroyed when they had attacked some children and also
caused trouble by chasing cyclists, narrowly avoiding
causing accidents. So, in addition to resentment against
his parents, he now harboured a grudge against his aunt
and uncle. Small wonder that by the age of eight he
already had a persecution complex and extended his
grudge to the whole world.

At ten years he became a juvenile offender, leading a
gang of other children in petty raids on various premises,
burglary, shoplifting and thefts from parked cars. He
was sent before the magistrates in the juvenile court
several times, who dished out first admonitions, then
more severe reprimands threatening him with loss of
liberty in an approved school, and finally approved school
itself. All this seemed to have little effect on young John.

Meanwhile he had become an avid reader, his favourite
books being accounts of the Chicago gangsters, which
fired his imagination to the point that he soon identified
himself with 'Legs' Diamond. He decided that he would
become a modern-day gangster. When he was eighteeen,
he bludgeoned an old man unconscious with a sand-filled

sock and robbed him of £10. For this he was sent unceremoniously to Borstal.

When he was released he set about finding some friends who would team up with him to form a gang. The youths, who were all unemployed like himself, would spend much of their time watching gangster films at the cinema in their home town of Worthing, Sussex, and John was particularly excited when a film of 'Legs' Diamond, his hero, was being shown. He saw the film five times. His friends thought he was what they called 'a fruit and nut case' on account of his obsession with the Chicago hoodlum.

One night they were drinking in one of the local pubs when John told them he intended to mastermind a bank robbery and wanted his two mates to take part in the raid with him. At first they demurred; it was too risky, they said. They would rather be free to play the pinball machines in the amusement arcades on the seafront than be locked up in prison. But in the end the persuasiveness of John Terry made them change their minds, and the trio planned to rob Lloyd's Bank in Durrington, a suburb of Worthing. 'It'll be a walkover,' John said. 'We'll be in Easy Street.' They decided to raid the bank on the morning of 10 November 1960.

On 8 November they called at a gunsmith's in Chiswick, where they purchased a handgun and fifty cartridges for five guineas. They then stole a car. It is incredible that the gunsmith did not think it suspicious that three youths should come into his shop to buy a gun ...

Terry drove his partners in crime to the home of his girlfriend Valerie Salter, at 2 Western Row, Worthing. They arranged to go to the bank from there on the morning of 10 November and be ready to move in as soon as the bank opened for business.

On the day of the crime Andrew Barker, a cashier, was behind the counter at 10 a.m. as the bank opened, getting ready for the morning's work. In a rear room a security guard named Henry Pull, aged sixty-one, was making tea. At this point two young men entered the bank and made for the end of the counter where Barker was counting banknotes. Just then the security guard emerged from the inner room, carrying a teapot in one hand.

The security guard approached one of the two men, raising a hand as though to speak to him. The man raised a gun he was carrying and shot the guard at close range through the eye. The teapot clattered to the floor as Henry Pull fell face down to the floor. Barker was later to testify that he heard the second man ask the gunman, 'Where's the money?' to which the gunman replied, 'It's in that bag.' The man then went to the end of the counter and grabbed a Gladstone bag which lay there. He then started towards the door.

A somewhat strange incident then took place. Barker related that he called out to the man, 'No, not that one.' The man then returned, threw the bag on the floor and picked up a large attaché case to which the clerk was pointing. The two men then both left the premises.

It was not long before the police had a good lead on the robbery. John Terry's two associates, Alan Hosier, who like Terry was twenty, and Philip Tucker, aged sixteen, hailed a passing taxi to escape, while Terry drove the getaway car to Valerie Salter's house. The plan had been to split up in this manner to facilitate their escape. But the taxi-driver was suspicious on being offered ten shillings and told to keep the change, for a half-crown fare. He reported the incident to the police, with a full description of his two passengers, who were rounded up within half an hour of the robbery.

While on his way to the girl's house in Western Row, Terry actually witnessed his two partners being rounded up by the police on the seafront and bundled into a police car. Terry told Valerie to pack a bag without further ado as they had to leave for Scotland to escape the law. He abandoned the stolen car, and the two of them took a bus to Littlehampton, where they hired a mini-cab to Portsmouth. They were stopped several times at road blocks, but since the police were looking for two men, they were not aware that a woman was involved, and the couple went on their way unsuspected.

From Portsmouth the two fugitives took a train to

Euston, and from there to Glasgow. Terry told the girl that they could be married at Gretna Green and that he would be purchasing a house for them with the money he had stolen from the bank, all of which he had in his possession before he had had an opportunity of sharing it out with his partners – if, indeed, he had any such intention. He had found more than £1,000 in the attaché case, £968 of which he handed to the girl for safe-keeping. It would look bad for him if he were what he called 'rumbled' and found with the money on him. As to the proposed Gretna marriage, they could certainly marry there, but what neither of them knew was that the romantic idea of an on-the-spot wedding over the anvil was a myth. This was no longer legal; the registrar had to be present, and the parties both had to wait out a twenty-one day residential qualification after giving notice of their intention to marry. Terry was twenty and the girl eighteen, so there was no age problem requiring consent.

But 'rumbled' he was, and it was John Terry's obsession with 'Legs' Diamond that proved his undoing. He had registered with the Glasgow hotel as 'Mr L. Diamond and Mrs Diamond'. Soon after they moved in, the hotel proprietor became suspicious of the 'honeymoon couple', Mr and Mrs Diamond, who had hardly any luggage to speak of and wore what could hardly be described as their best clothes, as would be expected of a newlywed couple. The 'groom' wore a bomber jacket and jeans, and the 'bride's' going-away outfit had seen better days. She wore no hat or gloves, which were usually worn with such an outfit.

Then the proprietor saw the photograph of John Terry in his daily newspaper. The manhunt had been extended to all parts of the British Isles. John Terry's portrait was the spitting image of 'Mr L. Diamond' ... The police were called, and the couple were arrested in their room, Terry on a charge of murder in furtherance of theft, and the girl as an accessory.

*   *   *

The trial opened on 20 March 1961 at Lewes Assizes, in the same courtroom which had been the scene of several famous trials before this one, including those of John George Haigh, the 'acid bath' killer, described in Chapter 6; Norman Thorne, the 'chicken farm' murderer[1], and Dr Bodkin Adams.

The judge was Mr Justice Stable, and the jury consisted of eleven men and one woman. Mr Geoffrey Lawrence prosecuted, assisted by Mr Peter Crowder. John Terry was defended by Mr Alan King-Hamilton, with Mr John Boland as his junior. Alan Hosier was defended by Mr Malcolm Morris Braithwaite, QC; Valerie Salter by Mr William Hemming; and the juvenile offender, sixteen-year-old Philip Tucker, was defended by Mr Travers Christmas Humphreys, QC, assisted by Mr David Jessel Samuels. It was an impressive array of some of the best and most able barristers at law.

All four defendants had spent months on remand awaiting the trial, which was to last ten days. The case had aroused a high degree of public interest, and special seating arrangments were made in the courtroom to accommodate the Press and the public.

All four defendants pleaded not guilty as their charges were read out: Terry with capital murder in the furtherance of theft, Tucker and Hosier with murder, and Salter with harbouring and assisting Terry knowing that he had shot and killed Henry Pull.

Prosecutor Lawrence's first witness was Detective Sergeant Frederick Turner, who gave evidence that a search of Salter's house had yielded the bolt of a gun, fourteen live cartridges and a man's bloodstained overcoat. A forensic expert, Dr Lewis Nicholls from Scotland Yard's Forensic Laboratory, of which he was at the time the director, testified that the gun was a cheap 9 mm gun of continental make, and that each cartridge contained about 110 pellets. 'At close range,' he stated, 'such a gun would be lethal against exposed parts of the body.' Having tested the weapon, Dr Nicholls stated that the fatal shot had been fired from a distance of six to nine inches. The gun had no safety mechanism, but his conclusions were that there was no way in which it could have gone off accidentally.

The next witness was Andrew Barker, the bank clerk, who described the raid. The prosecutor then asked Barker why he had called the man back and told him he had taken the wrong bag. 'That would seem a rather peculiar thing to do, would it not?' he asked.

Barker replied: 'It occurred to me that if the man discovered he had taken only an empty bag, the consequences might not have been too pleasant.'

'In other words. you wanted to get rid of him at all costs?' the judge intervened. 'I must say I am not surprised.'

Mr Christmas Humphreys put it to Barker that he had not in fact heard Tucker say, 'Where's the money?' and Barker replied. 'I do not agree with that.'

The prosecution's final witness was Detective Superintendent Maurice Ray, a fingerprint expert from Scotland Yard, who testified that he found two prints similar to Terry's on the trigger of the murder weapon.

The evidence against Terry was irrefutable. He had been positively identified by Andrew Barker, the bank clerk, and his fingerprints had been found on the gun. In the face of such indisputable evidence there was little that Terry's counsel could do beyond making a plea for leniency for his client.

Mr King-Hamilton began his defence by outlining Terry's disturbed childhood and the background which had contributed to his antisocial adolescent behaviour. It would be pointless to deny the charges, and he did not dispute the fact that his client had organized a planned raid on the bank with his two confederates. Mr King-Hamilton explained that Terry believed himself to be possessed by the spirit of the gangster 'Legs' Diamond, and suffered from hallucinations and other symptoms of schizophrenia. His plea would therefore be one of not guilty by reason of insanity.

Terry's counsel went on to say that it was known that the defendant had taken drugs, though it could not be proved that he was under the influence of any drug when he carried out the robbery. Terry had had eleven jobs, and had been sacked from several of them for taking drugs. He was a frequent user of Drinamyl, usually called 'Purple Hearts' by addicts. None of the other three defendants had been known to take them.

Philip Tucker, the juvenile defendant, came from a respectable hard-working family from what Mr King-Hamilton called 'the middle class', and had no record of previous offences. Alan Hosier came from a similar background and also had no criminal record. The girl defendant, too, had never been in trouble with the police, and was said to have 'an excellent character' before teaming up with the self-styled 'gang'.

Doctors and psychiatrists called by the defence now testified as to Terry's mental state, in an attempt to boost the defence case of diminished responsibility. Dr Arthur Patterson, in charge of psychiatry at the West London Hospital, stated that he had seen the accused after his arrest and it was his opinion that Terry was suffering from schizophrenia and was not responsible for his actions.

Asked by Mr King-Hamilton whether, in his opinion, Terry was insane at the time he committed the murder, Dr Patterson replied that although he was suffering from diminished responsibility, yet he knew what he was doing and he knew that what he was doing was wrong, so he was not insane in the legal sense.

Mr Geoffrey Lawrence, for the prosecution, then called psychiatrists in rebuttal of this opinion. A Dr Pearce and a Dr Dalziel had both examined the accused, and apart from agreeing that he had a mania for guns, both were adamant that he was sane. Dr Francis Brisby, then Principal Medical Officer at Brixton Prison, where Terry had been held pending the trial, stated that he had found no evidence of mental defect or any disease of the mind which would diminish the defendant's responsibility, and he agreed with the considered opinion of the two doctors who had preceded him in the witness-box.

The other three defendants were then called to give evidence on their own behalf. Tucker told the court that on the way to the bank Terry had sat 'fiddling with the gun' and repeated several times: 'I'm the fastest man in Texas.' He stated that Terry had assured them both that the gun would not be loaded.

Tucker was then questioned by Mr Justice Stable: 'Tell me – what do you think a bank guard should do when two young men go into a bank and one of them is holding a gun?'

Tucker replied: 'He should not have done anything – he was being held up.'

The judge then asked Tucker whether, according to this, he considered that the bank guard's being shot was therefore his own fault.

'No, you cannot say it was all his own fault,' Tucker replied. 'If we had not gone into the bank, he would not have been dead.'

Alan Hosier next went into the box and confirmed Tucker's statement that Terry had assured them that the gun was not loaded but would be used only to frighten the bank staff into handing over money. He told the court how Terry, whom he had known for about six years, had telephoned him to ask him whether he would be interested in earning £200 'to drive a car'. Fearing that it concerned something illegal such as drug-smuggling, he refused. However, he changed his mind later when he met Terry, who explained that the plan was to rob a bank and that he (Hosier) would be receiving a cut of the takings in addition to the £200 for driving the getaway car. After Terry had told him that there would be no violence, he agreed to drive the car.

After purchasing the gun and stealing the car in London, Terry loaded the gun as they drove back to Worthing, and fired it into a hedge. At this point, Hosier testified, he reminded Terry of their agreement, to which Terry had replied, 'It's OK. I'm just testing it to make sure it's for real and not a toy.'

The statement continued to the effect that they had reached Salter's house early on the morning of 10 November and that they had gone to the bank from there, Tucker driving the car. During the robbery he (Hosier) had stayed at the wheel of the car, which had been parked in a side street. A short while later he heard what sounded like 'a thud' and which he later realized could have been the muffled sound of a gunshot – muffled because it came from inside a building. Almost immediately afterwards, Terry and Tucker came running round the corner and jumped into the car, which he (Hosier) then drove off at speed. 'What happened?' he asked. To which Terry replied, 'The security guard got hold of the gun and it went off, but I don't think it hit him.'

Hosier continued by telling the court that he then panicked and took a wrong turning. They decided to split up and abandon the car. Terry went off to Valerie's house, while he and Tucker hailed a passing taxi and went off in the direction of their homes in the town. They told the driver to let them off several streets away from their respective homes, deciding to walk the remainder of the way, in order to divert attention from their addresses. It was as they were walking along that the police had picked them up after the tip-off from the taxi-driver.

Valerie Salter was next to be examined in the witness-box. Sobbing uncontrollably most of the time, she first related how she had met Terry and gradually fell under his spell. She knew that he used drugs, and thought that she might be able to influence him to give them up and settle into a more steady existence and find a job he could keep. She admitted that she had been told about the plan to rob a bank, and that Terry had told her that they would have a lot of money and be able to marry and have their own house.

When Mr Lawrence asked her why she had not immediately gone to the police, she replied, 'I don't believe it is a criminal offence to rob a bank.' The prosecutor was dumbfounded by this reply – so much so, that he had to ask her to repeat it. Asked why she thought so, she said that a bank had thousands of pounds and they were insured anyway, but she thought it would be a criminal offence to rob a poor person who had only a few pounds to live on. There was an audible rustling in the court, but this soon subsided and the judge did not need to intervene.

Valerie went on to testify that soon after the raid Terry came to her house and told her to pack some things as they would have to escape to Scotland, but they could be married as soon as they got there, and could then look for a house.

Asked why she went with Terry, knowing him to have committed the robbery, she replied in a low voice, 'I did not want to go, but I could not help myself.' At this point the judge asked her, 'You were so infatuated with him that you would have gone anywhere with him?'; to which she replied in the affirmative.

When they reached Portsmouth, she asked Terry whether it was true that a security guard had been shot. Terry said, 'Yes, but I never intended killing anybody. The guard grabbed the gun, and it just went off.'

The judge here intervened: 'Were you deeply in love with the defendant?' and Valerie replied, 'Yes, I was.'

In the course of the final cross-examination, Mr Malcolm Morris, for Hosier, emphasized that his client never went into the bank and did not see the guard killed. Mr Christmas Humphreys also pointed out that Tucker never suspected that Terry would fire the gun. He said that Tucker was a gullible young boy, four years younger than either of the two men and two years younger than the girl.

For Valerie, Mr Hemming pointed out that Terry had the pseudo-sophistication of a young man from London, and his offer to her of all those things that a young woman desires, marriage and a home of her own, had blinded her to his true character – that of a young man with a criminal record who was quite prepared to commit armed robbery and murder to further his aims.

Mr Justice Stable here interpolated: 'From the legal standpoint, the only matter to be taken into consideration is whether this defendant knew that Terry had fired a shot and, if she knew that a murder had been committed, whether she did anything to assist him in escaping from justice.'

In his final speech for the prosecution, Mr Geoffrey Lawrence described Terry as 'the mastermind' behind the robbery. 'At all stages,' he said, 'Terry was in control. The raid … was carefully planned over a long period.'

Mr Justice Stable, in his summing-up, went over all the various aspects of the evidence, pointing out to the jury that people's lives rested upon their decisions. The evidence, he said, had to be considered against each of the accused separately. The judge gave lengthy explanations to the jury of the law as it applied to the case, and reminded them also of the importance of each defendant's evidence as it related not only to themselves but to the others. He stressed that the jury's decisions must be based on this evidence and not on their feelings about the four accused.

The jury took two and a half hours to reach their verdicts. They found Terry guilty of capital murder in the furtherance of theft, for which he was sentenced to death. Hosier and Tucker were found guilty of murder. Hosier received life imprisonment, while Tucker, as a juvenile, was sentenced to be detained during Her Majesty's pleasure. Salter was found guilty of being an accessory, and placed on probation for a year.

Before passing sentence on the four defendants, the judge asked that the girl be brought back before him. She trembled in the dock as he turned towards her.

'You are not going to be sent to prison,' he said, 'for I do not believe that you have the slightest guilt in connection with the robbery at the bank. I do not believe that, when you set out for Portsmouth, you knew that the bank guard had been murdered. You found that out only when you reached Portsmouth.' Valerie nodded, then burst into tears.

'Go home,' the judge said, 'and start a new life with your family and friends. Your love for this young man was genuine, but it was misplaced. He was an unworthy object for your affections, and in time this experience will fade and you will find someone more worthy of you.' Sobbing, she was led from the court.

John Terry appealed, but his appeal was dismissed, and he was hanged on 26 May 1961. There was an anti-hanging demonstration outside the prison, and the leading campaigners against capital punishment, headed by Sir Sidney Silverman, MP, protested to the Home Secretary (Mr R.A. Butler), but to no avail.

Before he died, John Terry was informed that a sixteen-year-old girl whom he had known before he met the girl who stood trial with him for murder, had given birth to a son of whom he was the father. The boy was later adopted.

Note

1. For a description of this case see Georgina Lloyd, *With Malice Aforethought* (Robert Hale, 1989).

15

The Moat Farm Murder

Samuel Herbert Dougal (1903)

It seems strange to visualize an educated spinster of fifty-five, accomplished in the arts of music and painting, falling victim to the dubious charms of a ruthless conman. One could more easily imagine a young girl being bewitched by the blandishments of such of rogue – a young girl with little or no experience of the world. But Miss Camille Holland was not, it seems, so worldly-wise as her age and background would have suggested.

She was the daughter of a Frenchwoman who married a businessman from Liverpool. Born in India, she was sent to a select girls' boarding-school, of which her aunt, Sarah, was headmistress. When Camille reached school-leaving age, her aunt simultaneously retired from her headship of the school, and her erstwhile pupil became her companion-housekeeper until Aunt Sarah died in 1893, leaving everything to her niece. Camille Holland thus became heiress to about £6,000 in investments – a fortune in those days – plus all her aunt's jewellery, furniture and other assets.

In her early adult years Camille led a virtuous life. She met a young naval officer during the First World War, but he was drowned in a boating accident. After his death she always wore his cornelian ring, and her affection for him was obviously much deeper than anyone had imagined, for she forsook any idea of marriage. Mourning the young man who would have been her husband, she remained a virgin. She was a good practising Catholic and attended church regularly, and obtained a new position as a lady's companion after her aunt's death. She buried her grief in a busy life, attending to the needs of her elderly employer, and in her free time playing the piano, singing and composing songs, writing the words as well as the music. She also painted watercolours of flowers and still-life subjects. In time the memory of her youthful love receded, but she was eminently respectable and avoided the company of those men who were 'only after one thing', as the saying goes.

Thus it was that her sudden and unexpected infatuation for a 52-year-old married man, extending even to going away with him and living with him as his wife without the benefit of wedlock, astonished her friends, who wondered aloud what could have wrought this drastic transformation. It seems that she met him at the Earls Court Exhibition of 1898.

Samuel Herbert Dougal was a coarse, loudmouthed Cockney, a tall, heavily built and even more heavily bearded figure with a fondness for strong drink, pungent-smelling tobacco and the attentions of women of all ages, classes and social levels. A less likely candidate for the affections of the demure and respectable Miss Holland would have been hard to find. It is, indeed, hard to understand how she could have gone overboard for him in such a fashion. According to his many female admirers, he was said to have a kind of animal magnetism, a masculine vitality, which was their undoing. The number of young girls who succumbed to his apparent attractions was legion, as the large number of his illegitimate children bore witness. He certainly had a fatal attraction for Miss Holland – literally as well as metaphorically.

Dougal was born in Bow, in London's East End, in May 1846. His education was the most basic, after which he became an apprentice to a firm of civil engineers. This, however, was far too humdrum a job to suit a man of such extrovert personality, so he joined the Army, enlisting in the Royal Engineers at Chatham on 6 March 1866. He remained in the service for twenty-one years, serving in Ireland, Wales, and finally Nova Scotia for the last ten years. His service career ended on 22 March 1887 with the rank of quartermaster-sergeant, and he was said to have been an exemplary soldier.

His domestic life, however, was far from exemplary. In 1869 he married a Miss Griffiths. She bore him four children, but her married life was very unhappy, for Dougal was constantly drunk, abused her and kept her short of money. For sixteen years she put up with his constant ill-treatment, until in June 1885, towards the end of his army service in Nova Scotia, she suddenly fell ill, dying in twelve hours. Her death was attributed to food poisoning caused by oysters.

Two months later he married another woman, who seemed to have, like her predecessor, a liking for oysters ... and died in October after a bout of violent vomiting which was again attributed to the effects of the shellfish. She was hastily buried less than twenty-four hours later. As both these deaths occurred in military quarters, they were not required to be registered with the civil authorities of Halifax, Nova Scotia.

1887 was the year of Queen Victoria's Golden Jubilee. It was also the year in which Dougal's regiment returned to England. Dougal brought with him another young girl, but although she was passed off as his wife, they were not in fact married. She obviously was so besotted with him that she imagined that he had honourable intentions and would marry her in England. She gave birth to a child, but soon afterwards left him and returned to her parents in Halifax with her baby, to escape the constant beatings and abuse he meted out to her. She called herself a widow, to spare her parents embarrassment.

After his army service terminated, Dougal now turned his hand to a number of varied jobs, including those of salesman, storekeeper, the steward of the Stroud Green Conservative Club, surveyor, clerk, and publican. The pub was situated at Ware in Hertfordshire, which he ran in partnership with an elderly woman, using her money. After he had insured it and his house for a substantial sum, a fire occurred at both these premises, destroying them. On applying for the insurance money he was arrested; he was tried at St Albans for fraud in December 1889, but was acquitted for lack of evidence. He now moved to Dublin, where he met one Sarah White, marrying her on 7 August 1892. She bore him two children. The record does not state whether this lady was beaten or abused, but Dougal left her about two years after the wedding. He obviously had never heard of Dublin's famous oysters ...

Back in London, Dougal ran true to form. Instead of looking for a new job, he cast around for another woman to support him in the manner to which he had become accustomed, and who better than a Miss Emily Booty, whom he bumped into, literally, as she came out of a Camberwell bank, where she had been depositing an addition to her already substantial investments. She seemed to be very taken by the tall, bearded stranger, for very soon after this meeting they had leased and furnished a house – using Miss Booty's money, naturally – in Watlington, Oxfordshire.

Dougal now wrote to his estranged wife in Dublin, inviting her to come with her two children and live in 'his' house – we should really say that it was Miss Booty's house. Incredibly, his wife agreed to this most unsatisfactory situation, and it is indeed very hard to understand why a wife who had – presumably – been ill-treated by her husband should agree to come and live with her children in her husband's mistress's home with the mistress in residence. But come she did, and before long her younger child died – 'of convulsions', it was said. Dougal beat and abused his wife, so there is no reason to suppose that he had not done so when they had lived in Dublin. This time she decided to leave him and return to Dublin with the remaining child. She packed her belongings to this end, when her husband assumed a threatening attitude, and she called the police for her own and her child's safety.

While the police were there, the legal Mrs Dougal made her escape, and the officers decided to search the house, where they found a number of Miss Booty's possessions, which she had complained had gone missing, in Dougal's own private boxes and locked drawers. He was promptly arrested for larceny, and appeared at Oxford Quarter Sessions in April 1895. Owing to his unblemished army record, and his defence that Miss Booty had 'entrusted the items to him for safe-keeping' (Miss Booty was not in court to deny this), he was acquitted. Miss Booty, meanwhile, was hastily selling the house and moving her furniture and other belongings to a less insecure location. She was also understandably fed up with Dougal's various unorthodox goings-on.

It is not known exactly where Dougal lived after this – most likely in lodgings – but he did not have long to fend for himself before he was able to obtain rent-free accommodation at Her Majesty's expense. Having forged the signature of Lord Frankfurt on a cheque in Dublin, he was sentenced to twelve months' hard labour. During this time he feigned insanity and was taken to an establishment then known as a lunatic asylum, but the doctors there were not to be hoodwinked and after a short period of observation they pronounced him sane. He then served the remainder of his sentence in Pentonville prison.

Discharged in December 1896, he found himself unable to obtain work. He was fifty, had served a prison sentence, and had lost his army pension as a result. He appealed to his brother Henry, who lived at Biggin Hill in Essex. Henry managed to secure a job for him, doing clerical work, and also gave him rooms in his own house. Dougal managed to keep the job for over a year, but Henry was becoming somewhat disillusioned by the immoderate behaviour of his house guest. First of all, Mrs Dougal returned to him from Dublin once again with Olive, her surviving child, and once again Dougal beat and abused her, and she fled for what was to be the final time. Not even her husband's alleged 'animal magnetism and masculine vitality' could prevail upon her to endure any more of this ill-treatment. Then, when they had gone, Dougal began bringing various women to the house, quite blatantly and without any attempt to do so in an underhanded manner. It all became too much for Henry, who threw him out bag and baggage. He left his clerical job and moved back to London.

It was there, in September 1898, that he met the ill-fated Camille Holland at the Earls Court Exhibition. At the time she was lady's companion to an elderly widow, Miss Florence Pollock, who lived at 37 Elgin Crescent in the then fashionable Bayswater district. Posing as 'Captain Dougal, RE', he called upon the lady at this address in gentlemanly fashion, on two occasions, presumably to discuss financial matters – no opportunity for hanky-panky in such a genteel establishment. But they did manage to go off for a weekend at the Royal Hotel, Southend, as 'Captain and Mrs Dougal', which was the nearest the unfortunate lady ever got to having herself so described in any register. She was indiscreet enough to have told all her friends about this escapade, referring to Dougal as 'my sweetheart', and her friends were horrified. Whatever could have got into her?

What had got into her was, no doubt, the realization that at fifty-six this would probably be her last chance of a belated marital happiness and security, which she had, albeit subconsciously, yearned for all her life, ever since the death of her young naval officer, in the days of their youth long past. Years of repression of all her natural instincts had caused them to burst their bonds, throwing her Victorian modesty, virtue and propriety to the winds, at the advent of this plausible and unscrupulous rogue.

Back from Southend, Dougal rented a furnished house called Parkmoor, in Hassocks, Sussex, for £6 a month. It was conveniently near to Brighton, he pointed out – a town which Miss Holland was fond of visiting. Miss Holland provided the money for the rent of the house, and paid for the trips to Brighton in a hired pony-trap. She fondly hoped that marriage would be forthcoming soon. By now it was December; on the 2nd he had rented the house, and on the 5th Miss Holland left Mrs Pollock's house to travel to Brighton, ostensibly on her honeymoon. 'We were under the impression,' Mrs Pollock was to say later, 'that Miss Holland was going away to be married.'

The couple spent Christmas and New Year at Parkmoor, and it was during this time that Dougal persuaded Miss Holland to part with the sum of £1,500 to purchase a farm.

The contract, in Dougal's name, was signed on 19 January 1899. The couple moved to Saffron Walden, Essex, taking lodgings in that town, in order to be close to their new property, Moat Farm, Quendon, near Clavering, between Saffron Walden and Audley End, while arrangements were being made to finalize the legal transactions, refurbish the house and fetch Miss Holland's furniture from storage in London. The landlady at their lodgings at 4 Market Row, Saffron Walden, a Mrs Henrietta Wicken, was later to say that 'the couple seemed to be devoted to each other.' On 27 April the farmhouse was ready, and Mrs Wicken saw off her lodgers as they were driven to their new home in a pony and trap.

The neat, compact farmhouse was surrounded by a wide moat, crossed at only one point by a little bridge. Fir trees and an apple orchard screened the house from the road, in an isolated part of a remote, sparsely populated area of the Essex countryside. The nearest house, Rickling Vicarage, was half a mile away. I cannot do better than quote Miss F. Tennyson Jesse's description of the house from her book on this case in the *Notable British Trials* series:

> The house itself is a building that on a sunny day holds something sinister and dreary, a look as of a house in some wild Brontë tale, and that on a wet, grey day might stand for the epitome of everything that is lonely and grim ... Surrounded by dark fir trees and gnarled apple trees in a very ecstasy of contortion, it is a small, neat, almost prim house, its deeply sloping roof patterned in diamond shapes with lighter tiles; its famous moat circles it so completely that it is only possible to enter it at one point, where a bridge spans the water ...[1]

Two days after the couple moved in, Miss Holland engaged a seventeen-year-old maidservant, who left precipitately after a week, it would seem to escape her employer's 'husband's' attentions. Another girl was hired, also seventeen, and a day or two later Dougal tried to break into her room by forcing the lock. The new maid screamed for 'Mrs Dougal', who rescued her and took her to one of the guest bedrooms. 'I was only going to wind up the clock,' was Dougal's flimsy excuse. 'I wasn't born yesterday!' retorted Miss Holland. 'Any fool would know that you need the light to wind up a clock, so you would go in during the day while the girl was working, not try to break in at night and have to light a candle.' It seemed that Miss Holland was at last becoming wise to Dougal's womanizing habits, which he could not resist even under his own roof.

The girl promptly smuggled a letter out of the house to her mother, who came the next day to remove her. She also complained to Miss Holland, while her mother was present, that Dougal had sneaked up silently behind her earlier the previous day when she was alone in the kitchen and tried to kiss her, which she had vigorously resisted. The commotion had started Miss Holland's dog barking furiously, but when she came to investigate Dougal had slid out of the kitchen via the door into the garden, and the girl did not pursue the matter.

Miss Holland did not have time to seek and engage another maidservant, for three days after the hasty departure of the last one, she disappeared.

* * *

Conflicting stories were bandied about as to when Miss Holland had last been seen alive. Some averred that they had seen her being driven by Dougal in their pony and trap in the direction of Saffron Walden, but were vague about the time, or even which day. Others said they had seen her, alone, in that town. To those of his acquaintances who asked him where she was, Dougal replied that she had gone on a cruise with some friends of hers from London who had a large motor yacht. Few believed his explanation; who would move into a new farm property and then suddenly take off on a cruise? It just did not make sense.

Meanwhile Dougal was busy learning to forge Miss Holland's simple and unpretentious signature, and when he felt proficient enough at the job he began writing cheques on her account. Over the next two years he had acquired all her capital assets; the farm she had bought was already his. By September 1901 he had £2,912 15s 0d standing to his credit in a bank account in his own name. Thus enriched and no longer threatened by Miss Holland's presence, he got rid of all the livestock, dropping all pretence of being a farmer, and pursued the life of a country gentleman. He bought a car, the first ever to have been seen in that part of the country, and sold the pony and trap. Hunting, shooting, drinking, smoking expensive cigars, and attending the races were his convivial occupations – as well as, of course, unabated lechery, which age had not dimmed one whit. Servant girls followed one after another, their inevitable pregnancies making their work increasingly difficult. How many bastards he sired is a matter for conjecture; he certainly never kept count.

Rumours abounded in all the neighbouring villages about the goings-on at Moat Farm, which caused a scandal to the gentlefolk of the area. On 1 August 1902 he was divorced from his legal wife in Ireland, who wished to marry an engine-driver.

In September, when Kate Cranwell, another servant girl, went home to have a child, she filed a paternity suit for maintenance, which set the cat among the pigeons, for he chose to contest the suit and thus not only invoked the wrath of the wronged girl and her parents but also inspired the attentions of the law. Kate Cranwell's sister Eliza accused him openly in court of forging 'Mrs Dougal's' cheques during her absence. Local rumours added more fuel to the fire. The police began asking questions: where *was* the self-styled Mrs Dougal? On a cruise? Hardly likely. Cruises do not normally last so long.

In February 1903 the persistent rumours intensified. Women who had been in the house at Moat Farm reported seeing that many of the missing woman's possessions were still there: clothes hung in the wardrobes, and even such personal things as her mother-of-pearl handled hairbrush and comb set, with matching mirror, an amber perfume spray, and some items of jewellery, were still in her bedroom. Normally a lady going on an extended trip abroad would not go without such items. As for the story of a cruise, no one now believed it. There were some who thought that she might have left Dougal and gone away with another man, but when her friends in London and elsewhere were questioned, no one had heard from her for what was now getting on for four years. The police were not merely puzzled, they were by now seriously concerned, especially when they heard the rumour going the rounds that Dougal had killed her and buried her body.

It was decided to set up a investigation and find out what had really happened to the unfortunate Miss Holland. Her niece and nephew knew nothing; her solicitor likewise. This was not thought unusual, because they were accustomed to long silences from her, since she often used to travel and in any case was not a very enthusiastic letter-writer. So they had thought nothing of it, beyond thinking that the silence was perhaps a bit longer than usual. A police superintendent was sent to interview Dougal at Moat Farm, but found nothing suspicious in the latter's mien or conversation. He said simply that she had left him, that he had not heard from her at all, and that he did not know where she was. He admitted that the story of the cruise was an invention intended to spare him embarrassment. The superintendent later reported that he considered Dougal to be telling the truth, adding, 'I shook hands with him on leaving.'

Detective Inspector Bower, of Scotland Yard, and Detective Inspector Marden of the Essex Constabulary, together investigated the financial angle which was giving them grounds for concern. A cheque dated 28 August 1902, signed 'Camille C. Holland', was stated by her nephew, Ernest Holland, to be a forgery. 'That is definitely not my aunt's signature,' he said.

The day after the police visit, Dougal withdrew £605 from his bank and went to London with his latest maidservant, Georgina Cranwell, the sixteen-year-old sister of Kate, whose new baby by Dougal was a month old. Georgina was heavily pregnant ... They stayed at the Central Hotel in Long Lane for a week, afterwards returning to Moat Farm. On the Friday – the 13th – he moved out with a pile of baggage, staying that night again at the Central Hotel in Long Lane, where he was joined on the Saturday by Georgina Cranwell. She, too, had moved out of Moat Farm with a quantity of luggage, but she left this at Liverpool Street railway station left-luggage deposit. Dougal and his companion then travelled to Bournemouth for the weekend, staying at the Coburg Hotel. This was a long weekend, for they did not leave until the Tuesday, when they returned to London. Dougal remained there 'to attend to some business transactions'; he told Georgina to return to Moat Farm and wait for him there, saying he would be coming home 'in a few days', but without specifying exactly how long.

On Wednesday, 18 March, at about 1.30 p.m., Dougal entered the Bank of England in the city and presented fourteen £10 bills, asking the clerk to change them into smaller-denomination bills. The cashier, William Lawrence, spotted that the numbers of these bills were on a 'stop list' which had been issued to all banks. 'I am sorry, sir,' Lawrence said, 'but I must ask you to accompany me to the sub-manager's office.' On Dougal's asking him why this was necessary, the clerk replied that there was a query as to the numbers on some of the bills. He asked Dougal to endorse one of them with his name and address. Dougal wrote 'Sydney Domville', giving an address in Bournemouth.

As Dougal sat in the sub-manager's office, the police officer on duty at the bank was sent for. DI Henry Cox immediately confronted him with: 'You are Samuel Dougal. I must ask you to come with me to the police headquarters in Old Jewry.' Dougal simply said, 'Yes', and went quietly with the officer. As they approached Cheapside, Dougal suddenly made a run for it. Unfortunately for him, Frederick's Place, which he had sprinted into, was a cul-de-sac. DI Cox had no difficulty in recapturing him, assisted by a passing constable who saw the struggle.

At the police station Dougal was searched, and on him were found eighty-three £5 bills, eight £10 bills, £63 in gold sovereigns, a £5 gold coin, seven rings (one of these being the cornelian ring which Miss Holland had always worn), five watches and several items of Miss Holland's jewellery. He was charged with the cheque forgery which Miss Holland's nephew had drawn to police attention. This was a holding charge, for the police had by this time decided that Moat Farm might repay a thorough search ...

The following day, Thursday, 19 March, Dougal was taken to Saffron Walden police station, and the search of the farmhouse began under the supervision of DI Scott, who made his headquarters in the house, together with his team of detectives. They searched every inch of the farmhouse, but found nothing. They questioned Georgina Cranwell, whose child was expected in two months' time. They drained the moat, slithering and slipping waist-deep in the thick black ooze at the bottom, but again came up empty-handed. They were convinced that a body – Camille Holland's body – must be *somewhere*. But where? They dug up the entire garden which surrounded the house, again without result. During this time Dougal ranted and fumed in his police cell, threatening to sue them for the damage to his garden.

The police now began systematically digging up the entire area of the farm. Dougal was now threatening them with a lawsuit for £1,000 for the damage to the farm, but the police ignored him and kept digging. They were pretty sure that Dougal would be in no position to sue them for anything by the time they had finished digging ...

One day, in the midst of all this heavy and laborious work in the clay soil of Essex, rendered glutinous by the recent torrential rains, a report filtered through to them from a villager who suddenly recalled that soon after Dougal had moved into the farm he had ordered workmen to fill in a drainage ditch which led from the farmyard to the horse pond. This struck DI Scott as rather odd, so he switched operations to excavating this filled-in ditch. It was full of horse manure, sewage and black sludge – a most unsavoury job for the diggers. But it was the police spade work (*sensu strictu*) which paid off in the in end. The several days spent by the diggers wallowing in filth yielded at last the secret of Moat Farm. One of the diggers struck a hard object with his pitchfork. It turned out to be a lady's size 2 shoe. Miss Holland, a diminutive woman standing just 5 ft 2 in, had worn size 2 shoes on her tiny feet.

Miss Holland's feet looked far from dainty when she was disinterred from her shroud of black sludge. Her malodorous remains, fully clothed, were lifted from the grave on to a slab, which was placed across two chairs in one of the greenhouses pending identification by Mrs Wicken, who recognized the garments worn by the corpse, which included items she had stitched and altered herself. The buckled shoes, too, Mrs Wicken recognized immediately. Upon forensic examination, pathologists found the body to be in a fairly well-preserved condition, which they attributed to the quantity of blackthorn branches which had been laid on top of it.

Miss Holland had been shot at close range through the head with one bullet from a .22 revolver. The gun was proved to be one owned by Dougal, and the angle of firing, according to the pathologists, Dr Pepper, showed that it had been discharged from a gun held by a person in a higher position, physically speaking, than the victim. From this it could be inferred that Dougal had been sitting in his pony-trap and had shot Miss Holland as she stood on the ground with her back towards him. The bullet had entered behind the right ear and a few inches above it.

The unusually large quantity of clothing that the victim had worn at the time of her death also contributed, the pathologist stated, to the state of preservation of the body. Miss Holland had worn two pairs of woollen combinations, a pair of bloomers, steel-framed corsets, two camisoles, two petticoats, a dress, shoes and stockings. If Dougal had ostensibly been taking her for a ride in the trap in order to kill her on a remote part of the farm, it is likely that she would also have been wearing a hat and gloves, as was usual in those times for such an outing, but no hat or gloves were found. A lace handkerchief had been laid across the face of the corpse – a curious touch indeed from such a ruthless scoundrel.

Samuel Dougal was charged on Thursday, 30 April 1903, with 'wilfully, maliciously, feloniously and with malice aforethought' killing Camille Holland. The arrest took place in the dining-room of Moat Farm, and the inquest was held in the barn. Dougal was remanded before the magistrates several times, before finally being committed for trial on 29 May. While in prison he wrote several letters to the various women in his life, including his divorced wife, who had, apparently, given up the idea of marrying the engine-driver and instead had become a Roman Catholic nun, taking the name Mary Magdalene.

He made a bizarre suggestion to the mothers of his numerous offspring that they should band together and make an outing of coming to his forthcoming trial at Chelmsford. One such missive read as follows:

> I dare say the girls have received their notices ... to attend next Monday at Chelmsford, have they not? There will be several from about there, and it would be a good idea to club together and hire a trap and drive all the way. It is a delightful drive through undulating country, and at this time of year it would be a veritable treat for them all.

The mind boggles ...

The trial opened in the Shire Hall, Chelmsford, on 22 June before Mr Justice Wright. Mr C.F. Gill, KC, prosecuted, while the accused was defended by Mr George Elliott. Dougal protested his innocence, but no one was convinced, and no evidence was offered on his behalf. At 4.50 p.m. on the following day the judge gave his summing-up and the jury retired. They took seventy-five minutes to reach a unanimous verdict of guilty of murder. When he was sentenced to death, he made no reply.

Dougal appealed, but his appeal was dismissed. He thereupon wrote personally to the Home Secretary. In this letter he admitted that he had indeed shot Miss Holland, but maintained that the gun had gone off accidentally. He gave a long, involved and totally unconvincing explanation as to how he came to be holding the gun in the first place, considering that he stated that he and Camille had been 'returning home from Stansted, where they had been shopping'. He decided to bury her on the farm to avoid any awkward questions, and when he got home and the maid asked him where she was, he told her that she had gone to London. The Home Secretary's response is not on record, but he is most unlikely to have been impressed by this piece of fabrication.

Samuel Dougal was hanged in Chelmsford Prison on 8 July 1903. He was fifty-seven. It is said that he confessed his guilt to the prison chaplain just moments before he met his ignominious end.

Camille Holland lies buried in Saffron Walden churchyard, her grave headed by a stone cross on which is carved the figure of an angel with a young girl. The inscription states that she 'died, aged 56, under distressing circumstances'.

Note

1. F. Tennyson Jesse, *The Trial of Samuel Dougal*, Notable British Trials series, ed. Harry Hodge (William Hodge, London).

16

The Rugeley Poisoner

Dr William Palmer (1856)

We have to go back in time more than one hundred and thirty years to peruse the career of William Palmer, who has been dubbed the Prince of Poisoners by his biographers, and who certainly had an indefatigable propensity for dispensing lethal drugs to men, women and children indiscriminately as it suited his purposes.

Palmer was a doctor, the son of a wealthy widow in Rugeley, Staffordshire. Following the custom of the day, his parents had decided that he should become a surgeon, and as little more than a boy he was apprenticed to a firm of apothecaries and wholesale drug merchants, which conducted a large proportion of its business by mail order. Since the young William Palmer was not yet of an age to be given the responsibility of dispensing drugs, he was put in charge of the postal section.

After only a few months, the firm discovered that the mail order department sales were falling off at an alarming rate, but could discover no apparent reason for this. A little later, however, dissatisfied customers started writing to the firm asking why they had not received a receipt for the cash they had forwarded or, in some cases, the goods they had ordered. Inquiries were made, and eventually young William confessed that he had pocketed the money. He was dismissed immediately, and his mother made good the losses.

By the age of eighteen, his father having died in the meantime, William was forced to realize that he must do something to salvage his career. Despite the gossip in

Rugeley, Mrs Palmer managed to get her wayward son another apprenticeship, this time to a surgeon, a Mr Tylecote. However, this was to be another short-lived introduction to medical studies; Mr Tylecote had been imprudent enough to keep his patients' fees in a cardboard box in the surgery ...

Mrs Palmer again made up the losses, but Mr Tylecote refused to have William back, and the light-fingered young student ended up as a medical college freshman, probably after his influential mother had pulled a few strings on his behalf; he certainly could not have had good references from his two previous employers.

Three years later, having completed the requisite studies, William went to London to take his finals as a surgeon at St Bartholomew's Hospital, gaining his qualifications in August 1846, after which he returned to Rugeley and set up in practice on his own account. However, it is a debatable point whether he had any serious intent of running a successful practice; notoriety had preceded him regarding not only his thefts from his two past employers but also an affair with one of Dr Tylecote's patients many years his senior, which was common knowledge, and also the outcome of a drinking contest in which he had challenged a man named Abley to drink a bottle of brandy at one go. Abley, who was already drunk, gleefully took up his challenge, after which he collapsed and died in the pub.

The coroner, at the inquest on Abley, commented harshly on William's behaviour, implying that he was, in effect, responsible for the man's death. This attitude was reinforced by the fact that it also emerged at the inquest that William had been carrying on an affair with the wife of the deceased. But if the widow had imagined that her youthful lover would now marry her, she was doomed to disappointment; nothing was further from his mind, and in fact after Abley's death he dropped her like the proverbial hot brick.

With all the gossip about him, it certainly seems odd that he would have returned to Rugeley if he had had the slightest intention of carrying on more than a desultory token medical practice; he would have been very optimistic if he had imagined that many patients would come to a doctor with such a dubious reputation. What seems more than likely is that he was attracted back to his home town by the presence of his numerous friends and acquaintances among the racing fraternity. For some considerable time he had been an avid follower of 'form' and had been placing bets (mostly unsuccessful) funded by his indulgent but misguided mother, whose proximity and willingness to bail him out when the non-payment of his betting debts threatened trouble must have made Rugeley doubly attractive.

Early in 1847 he met a Miss Annie Thornton, who was reputed to have a sizeable fortune. The opportunist William lost no time in courting her, and the young couple were married. Only after the marriage was the bridegroom made aware that Annie's fortune was vested in trustees and that Annie was a ward in Chancery. Her mother came to stay with the young couple, and William soon discovered that, since Annie's father was dead, on the death of her mother she would come into possession of her inheritance. This knowledge was tantamount to signing Mrs Thornton's death warrant. Within a week of her arrival William's unsuspecting mother-in-law fell ill with severe stomach pains, vomiting and diarrhoea. William treated her with medicines which the patient stated 'tasted vile', but she did not improve and he declared himself not satisfied with the progress she was making and called in a second opinion. This was a Dr Bamford, at that time aged seventy-five and doddering. He diagnosed gastric fever and prescribed various pills and potions, but Mrs Thornton grew rapidly worse and within another week she was dead.

According to the law in those days, William now had full control of his wife's fortune, and he saw no reason to over-exert himself building up his medical practice. So, while Annie dutifully stayed at home, ran the house and bore him five children in as many years, four of whom died before they were a year old, her husband hot-footed it to the pubs and racecourses with the brotherhood of the turf.

By the time William had been married for three years he

had to all intents and purposes given up his medical practice, which was a mere sham behind the brass plate which adorned his imposing house, situated opposite the Talbot Hotel, his favourite hostelry. He spent most of his time at the racecourses of the area, interspersed with sessions in the taverns, but not even the fortune which his late father-in-law had left his wife could withstand such a consistent degree of depletion, and by 1850 he was unable to meet his obligations and was barred as a defaulter at Tattersall's. He therefore now had to conduct his turf commissions through a nominee, or persuade one of his cronies to accept his bets, backed by some plausible-sounding agreement. It was well known in racing circles that William's wealthy mother had come to his rescue, and his creditors had no reason to doubt that she would do so again in the future if necessary.

One such man was a Mr Bladon, who had known William in his more prosperous days. On the strength of the latter's persuasiveness and his own belief that, at worst, the old lady would pay up if bets were lost, Bladon allowed William to place bets with him, and before the season was half-way through William owed him £800. Bladon was, understandably, annoyed that such a debt had been run up in such a short time and, moreover, that William had made no attempt even to reduce it. He threatened to come to Rugeley and expose William to his friends.

If he had imagined that a cash settlement would have been immediately forthcoming as a result of these tactics, Bladon was disappointed. Instead, William replied by return, explaining that it was only 'a matter of two or three days' before he would be in a position to settle the debt in full, and inviting Bladon to come and stay with him in Rugeley until the money was repaid. Nothing could have been more open and above-board. The unsuspecting Bladon, disarmed by this apparently friendly gesture, arrived in Rugeley, where he was entertained by Dr Palmer and his wife, and joined in the convivial evenings at the Talbot Hotel and other inns, reproaching himself meanwhile for having ever doubted his host's honesty.

Three days later he was taken ill with violent vomiting and paroxysms of cramp. Before any of his relations even knew of his illness he was dead (a death certificate was produced by the aged Dr Bamford) and hastily buried.

Before his death Bladon had mentioned to some of his friends that Palmer owed him £800, and afterwards the dead man's relations approached Palmer with a view to his repaying the debt. Palmer denied that there had ever been such a debt. The denial convinced nobody, but since Dr Bamford's death certificate had stated unequivocally that the unfortunate Bladon had died from gastric enteritis, and since a 'bug' had been going around the area, albeit not fatally, no suspicion attached to Palmer and no inquest was called for.

Palmer soon found, however, that no one would have any dealings with him except on a ready-money basis – and there was no ready money. His wife's fortune had been dissipated, and his mother was becoming more and more unwilling to advance her son money. It was bad enough, she reasoned, that her son was a compulsive gambler, who would continue to place bets, win or lose; but that was no reason for her to squander her resources and lay herself open to future destitution. It was time to call a halt, and she told William so in no uncertain terms.

There was no alternative but to have recourse to moneylenders, and Palmer contacted two such men named Pratt and Padwick, who conducted their transactions almost exclusively with the patronizers of the turf. He found that they were willing to lend him money if he gave them postdated bills which had to be countersigned by his mother.

Palmer had already not only murdered Bladon and his mother-in-law but also despatched the babies which his numerous girlfriends produced so inconveniently, in order to avoid having to pay out on affiliation orders. The usual method was to dip a finger into a solution of a deadly poison and offer it to a hungry infant to suck. In the mid-nineteenth century infant deaths were so commonplace as to arouse no suspicion – they were accepted as a fact of life. It is also within the bounds of possibility that Palmer had slipped a little something into the bottle of brandy that Abley drank, though this could not be proved. So, to a man who murdered without compunction as and when he deemed it would suit his purposes, the little matter of forging his mother's signature to the IOUs given to the two moneylenders was small beer indeed.

So, assuring Pratt and Padwick that the old lady had promised to honour her obligations if necessity arose, William returned in a couple of days or so with the bills, duly countersigned by Mrs Palmer – or so the moneylenders thought. Forgery had only recently been taken off the list of capital offences, but a long prison term was still the penalty. If his mother ever discovered what he was doing, William mused, she would still rather pay up than see her son a convict. So the money was advanced, and the young doctor, gripped inexorably in the gambling obsession, despite the fact that hardly a single bet was successful, doubled and trebled his stakes, in the vain hope born of desperation that somewhere, among the many contenders, there must be a horse which would prove its mettle and win against all odds. He was betting now in thousands rather than hundreds, and getting himself more and more inextricably bogged down in the morass of his self-destruction. By the end of 1853 his position was hopeless. Although Pratt and Padwick were not yet pressing him, Palmer was fully aware that next year their bills would fall due. And as if all this were not enough, a young girl from a respectable background who had been foolish enough to allow him to seduce her was now threatening to expose him. He found a doctor in Stafford who was willing to perform an abortion and somehow raked up the money to pay for it, so at least he managed to avert trouble from that quarter. But what of the financially bigger issues?

At the beginning of 1854 Palmer insured his wife Annie for the sum of £13,000. He had no difficulty in doing this, for Mrs Palmer was perfectly healthy and the insurance companies (he used more than one) knew him as a young country doctor with a wealthy mother – so wealthy, it seemed, that the doctor did not have to bother unduly with following his profession. Regrettable, perhaps, but it was not a crime. The insurance was effected with no questions asked.

All through the summer of 1854 Annie Palmer gradually declined, at first complaining only of a sore throat, then of an intolerable thirst. Then, from time to time, she would be sick and suffer from bouts of diarrhoea. Meanwhile Palmer was conducting an affair with the maidservant, Elizabeth Tharm, who was only fifteen at the time. And while she grew big with child, in the room adjoining hers Annie Palmer's symptoms rapidly worsened and she took to her bed, prostrated by incessant vomiting and distressing diarrhoea. On 29 September she died; Dr Bamford, now eighty-two, was called in to give the customary certificate stating that death was due to gastric enteritis and, no inquest having been deemed necessary, Mrs Palmer was buried.

Elizabeth Tharm's child was born a few months later. Palmer made no secret of the fact that the child was his.

The insurance companies, having no knowledge of other mysterious deaths that had occurred in Rugeley, paid out on the policies due on the death of Annie Palmer without quibble, and William was able to settle all his outstanding commitments in full. But, he realized, this was only maintaining the status quo; he would have to cast around for some other source of income if he were to maintain the style of living to which he had become accustomed. He could no more stop himself than a stone being rolled down a sloping cliff-top and plummeting to the rocks below. So he began to look round for another subject.

He did not have to look far. His brother Walter, an alcoholic, was drinking himself to death as fast as he could. If he were to go sooner rather than later, no one would be in the least surprised. But this time he would not content himself with a mere £13,000 – the value he had put on Annie's life. This time he would go for broke. The jackpot – £82,000.

This time, however, Palmer had overreached himself. The insurance companies, while not suspicious about Mrs

Palmer's death, were dubious as to his ability to pay the premiums due on such a vast sum. They knew nothing about Walter's alcoholism; indeed, they had been sent a medical certificate (written by the ever-obliging Dr Bamford – who else?) to say that Walter was what in insurance terms is known as 'a good life'. But, they insisted, £82,000 was far too much; and once again Palmer had to be content with £13,000. This he handed to Pratt to secure him an advance carrying sixty per cent interest, further secured by another series of bills on which Palmer had again forged his mother's signature as guarantor.

No one in Rugeley was in the least surprised when, during the summer of 1855, Walter's alcoholism took a turn for the worse and in August he died from what was stated to be delirium tremens. But, to Palmer's alarm and astonishment, the insurance companies refused to pay out on the policies, and had still not paid three months later. Palmer was desperate, thrashing about, metaphorically speaking, like a fish out of water. Pratt was pressing him for £11,500.

At this point in the story, John Parsons Cook enters the arena. He was a contemporary of Palmer's, two years his junior, and the two men had been friends for some time, both sharing the dubious distinction of having given up a decent professional career for the racetrack. Whereas Palmer had qualified as a surgeon, Cook had been articled to a solicitor, but abandoned the law when he came into a £12,000 inheritance and embraced the brotherhood of the turf. More ambitious than Palmer, he not only bet heavily, but he kept his own stable of racehorses, and it was the occasion of his mare Polestar winning the Shrewsbury Handicap that marked him as a victim for the pecuniary advantage of his friend.

On 6 November Cook came to Rugeley and stayed with Palmer, whose financial position, as we have seen, was perilous in the extreme. The insurance companies had refused to pay out on Walter's death (these policies were never paid) and in addition to the sum of £11,500 which he owed Pratt, Padwick had by now taken out a writ for £4,000 against him. Cook himelf had one great advantage over Palmer – he had good credit. If his mare Polestar won the big race, Palmer surmised, and Cook had backed her adequately (Palmer could not back her as he had neither cash nor credit), and Cook's winnings were in some way to find themselves in Palmer's hands, he could at least pay instalments on account to Pratt and Padwick and thus, at least temporarily, stave off impending disaster.

On Sunday, 11 November, Palmer and Cook left Rugeley and on arriving in Shrewsbury put up at the Raven Hotel. On the following day Cook proceeded to back Polestar, entering the transactions in his betting book, which he always carried with him.

The next day, Tuesday, saw Polestar run and win the race. Cook was jubilant; he pocketed £800 in cash from on-course bookies, and on settlement day at Tattersall's he would have £1,020 due to him for collection. He also took an IOU for a further £200. He celebrated his good fortune with Palmer at the Raven Hotel, where it was decided that they would say until the end of the race meeting on Thursday.

In the evening a Mrs Brooks who was staying at the hotel and who had previously been introduced to both Palmer and Cook was going up to her room on the first floor when she observed Palmer with a tumbler of liquid in his hand which he was holding up to the gas jet on the landing as though to examine the contents by its light, after which he went into his room. A moment later he reappeared, this time greeting Mrs Brooks as she walked along the landing. In his hand was the glass, which he told her contained brandy and water for his friend John Cook.

Soon after partaking of the brandy and water (plus whatever ingredient Palmer had added to it) Cook was violently sick, and continued vomiting on and off all night. According to the later evidence of Mrs Brooks, a number of people had been taken ill at that race-meeting in Shrewsbury and contaminated water was given as the cause. Cook appeared to be satisfied with this explanation, because he felt better the next day (15 November) and returned to Rugeley with Palmer, taking a room at the Talbot Hotel opposite Palmer's house. On the Friday (16

November) Cook and Palmer dined together, and in answer to questions Cook said that he had quite recovered from his indisposition at Shrewsbury. Between 9 and 10 p.m. Cook returned to the Talbot Hotel, where he was seen by the chambermaid, Lavinia Barnes, who was later to testify that he was perfectly sober.

At 8 a.m. the next day Palmer arrived at the Talbot Hotel, where he ordered a cup of coffee for Cook from another chambermaid, Elizabeth Mills, who took the coffee up to Cook in his room. Palmer was in the room with him: Cook in bed, Palmer sitting on a chair by the bedside. Miss Mills, in her evidence given later, said that she did not see Cook drink the coffee, but that when she returned to the room half an hour later to collect the tray, she observed that Cook had been vomiting, and that there was also a jug in the room that was not the property of the hotel. She attached no particular significance to this, and took it downstairs with the tray.

Cook, feeling very ill, stayed in his room, and Palmer said that he would arrange 'a light diet' for him. He had only to cross the road to reach his home; once there, he sent his cleaning woman, Anne Rowley, to bring a bowl of broth from a Mr Robinson's establishment further along the road. According to Mrs Rowley:

> Dr Palmer said that the broth was not hot, and he would warm it by the fire. He told me to go back to my work in the kitchen, and he would bring it to me there when it was hot enough, which he did. He told me to take it to the Talbot Hotel across the road for Mr Cook, and to see that he took a little bread with it. I was to tell the chambermaid this, of course, as I could not go myself into Mr Cook's room.

Anne Rowley gave the bowl of broth to Lavinia Barnes with her master's instructions, but Cook refused to partake of it, saying he was too ill to feel hungry. Lavinia Barnes sent Palmer a message to this effect. He replied that the sick man *must* take it, as it would do him good. This time Elizabeth Mills tried to induce him to take the broth, but again he refused. Elizabeth evidently thought it was a great pity that good food should be wasted, and took a couple of spoonfuls herself. Within half an hour she was violently sick and had to go to bed for the rest of the day.

Cook continued to be very poorly, and Palmer called in his old faithful standby, Dr Bamford. He said that Cook had a bilious attack caused by having had too much to drink the previous night. Cook was most indignant at this, protesting that he had been perfectly sober (as Lavinia Barnes would corroborate later). On Sunday Dr Bamford prescribed some pills containing calomel, rhubarb and a half-grain of morphia. Palmer, in the meantime, told Lavinia Barnes that he had to go to London the following day as he had some business to attend to.

In London, Palmer located a commission agent named Herring, with whom he had done business from time to time, and engaged him to collect Cook's winnings from Tattersall's on his behalf, since Palmer himself was barred from doing transactions with them as a defaulter. This amounted to £1,020, of which Herring was authorized by Palmer to pay £450 on account to Pratt and £350 to Padwick, and to retain £100 as his own commission. Since Palmer owed Herring a sum in unpaid commission considerably in excess of this, Herring did not pay Padwick but kept the £350, which still left a sum owing. Padwick was thus still unsatisfied, and Palmer would have been most alarmed had he known of Herring's duplicity, for Padwick still held a forged bill for £2,000 owing by Palmer.

During the course of the afternoon Palmer visited Pratt and paid him a further £50 on account. Thus, for the time being, Pratt was pacified. But – and this is the vital point – all these debts were being paid with Cook's money. Yet, with barefaced effrontery, Palmer visited Cook on his return to Rugeley that night: 'I saw him between eight and nine o'clock going upstairs to Cook's room,' Lavinia Barnes was to to testify later. A Mr Salt, a surgeon of Rugeley, also testified that Palmer came to his surgery at about nine o'clock that evening where he purchased three grains of strychnine. Mr Salt's assistant, a Mr Newton, stated that Palmer was not in the surgery more than two minutes.

A friend of Cook's who called in to see him that evening found Palmer in his room and Palmer had told him that he 'had to go home to give the servants some instructions for the next morning but that he would be right back'. Palmer was certainly seen later that night, probably between 10.30 and 11 p.m., going into Cook's room, where, it may be surmised, he found an opportunity to switch the calomel, rhubarb and morphia pills Dr Bamford had left for a more deadly concoction which Palmer had made up to resemble them in appearance, in the privacy of his surgery. He was also seen to leave the hotel towards midnight, having doubtless ensured that Cook had taken the pills and settled for the night.

It was just after midnight when Lavinia Barnes, clearing up for the night in the kitchen, heard the violent ringing of the bell from Cook's room. She rushed up the stairs and found Cook very ill, thrashing about in his bed and screaming in agony. He gasped that he was suffocating and sweat was beading his forehead. His symptoms seemed to come in paroxysms, and after one such bout he gasped out, 'Fetch Dr Palmer!' Miss Barnes sent the boot-boy to fetch him, and then went downstairs to the kitchen and told Elizabeth Mills to prepare a bowl of tepid water and flannels to cool the sick man's fever. In about five minutes Palmer arrived, and Miss Barnes went up to Cook's room with him. While there, she saw Palmer giving Cook a glass of a dark-coloured liquid to drink. Almost immediately Cook vomited.

Lavinia Barnes stayed in the room until Cook's symptoms began to subside and he was more composed, and she then withdrew and went to bed, at about one o'clock. Elizabeth Mills remained in the room with Palmer and the sick man until about three o'clock, when she, too, retired, leaving them together. She returned at about six o'clock to see how Cook was, and found that Palmer had left. Cook told her that the doctor had gone home at about a quarter to five. Asked how he was feeling, Cook told her 'no better and no worse.' When she asked him what he thought was the cause of his latest attack of sickness, he replied, 'I think old Dr Bamford's pills do not suit me – they are too strong. I have asked Dr Palmer to see that he prescribes me something else instead.'

Cook evidently had no suspicions, for later, at about midday, he rang his bell and asked Elizabeth Mills to send the boot-boy for Dr Palmer, and asked if he might have a cup of coffee. When she took up the coffee just after twelve o'clock, she found Palmer already in the room. He then asked her for a cup of coffee for himself, which she supplied. The inference is that Palmer somehow managed to slip something into Cook's coffee while the maid was in the kitchen preparing the second cup of coffee for Palmer.

What neither Cook nor the maid knew was how Palmer had been employed earlier that morning. Between eleven and twelve o'clock he had visited the pharmacy of a Rugeley chemist named Hawkins, with whom he had had no dealings for more than two years. He was attended to by a young apprentice named Roberts, and asked for two drachms of prussic acid, two drachms of Battley's solution of opium, and six grains of strychnine. One might have imagined that such a large purchase of lethal drugs would have given young Roberts pause for thought, but it transpired that the apprentice did not even record the transaction in the firm's books. He would probably have forgotten about it had not Newton, Mr Salt's assistant, appeared in the shop while Roberts was putting up the drugs. It will be remembered that only the previous evening Palmer had purchased three grains of strychnine from him, so the appearance on the scene of Mr Newton just now was more than an unfortunate coincidence – it was a positively dangerous situation.

While Roberts was occupied with the drugs, Palmer walked quickly across to Newton, grabbed him in jovial fashion by the shoulders and hustled him out of the door into the street. Newton naturally thought that Palmer had something of importance to tell him, which he wished to impart in private. He was therefore considerably surprised when Palmer launched merely into small-talk. While they were talking, a man named Bressington came up to

Newton, excused himself and tackled him about some bills which, he claimed, Mr Salt owed him. While they spoke, Palmer went back into the shop, paid for and collected his order and came out again before Newton and Bressington had finished their conversation. Newton thought Palmer's behaviour so odd that he asked young Roberts what Palmer had purchased, and eventually was able to give evidence about Palmer's purchase of strychnine from him the previous evening.

Meanwhile, back at the Talbot Hotel, Cook, who was feeling a little better, asked that a message be sent to a Dr Jones, who shared his lodgings in a nearby town, that he come to visit Cook. When Dr Jones arrived, Palmer was not in Cook's room. Later, however, he arrived, and Dr Jones examined Cook while Palmer was in attendance. Jones was in and out of the room for the rest of the afternoon, and noted that Cook seemed considerably improved, until he took a little bread and water; this, however, seemed to reactivate the vomiting.

At seven o'clock Dr Bamford was sent for and the three doctors held a medical conference around Cook's sick-bed. During this consultation, Cook informed them that he would not again take the pills Dr Bamford was prescribing as they made him sick. The three doctors did not like such an interruption from the patient during a consultation, so they adjourned to the landing outside, where Palmer proposed that Dr Bamford make up the pills as before, but not tell Cook what they contained, since Cook took such an objection to morphia.

To this course of action Dr Bamford agreed, and it was arranged that Palmer should pick them up from Dr Bamford's surgery later that night. Dr Jones agreed to stay with the patient, and accordingly a bed was made up for him in Cook's room and arrangements made for him to take his meals at the hotel. Cook had meanwhile settled more comfortably and the vomiting had ceased.

Much to Dr Bamford's surprise, when Dr Palmer called upon him later that evening for the pills he insisted that Dr Bamford write the directions for taking them on the lid of the box. Palmer had never asked for this to be done before and, since Palmer would be administering them himself, Dr Bamford thought it unnecessary. However, he did as he was asked and at about eleven o'clock Palmer took the pills to Cook – having had them in his possession for about forty-five minutes since obtaining them from Dr Bamford. As Dr Jones was to say later, 'Palmer opened the box in my presence and showed me the directions ... and as he did so he remarked, "That is an excellent hand for an old man of over eighty to write, is it not?" and I agreed that it was an excellent hand.' Since the date of the prescription was included in the directions, this would seem to have been an ingenious ploy on Palmer's part to establish that the pills had in fact been prescribed by Dr Bamford.

At first Cook demurred on being asked to take the pills, but eventually he took them and immediately afterwards the vomiting recurred. After this had abated, Cook was persuaded to take a little bread and water to settle his stomach, and said that he would try to sleep. Dr Jones then went downstairs to the dining-room for a late supper, and Palmer went home. At about midnight or just after, Dr Jones returned to Cook's room to retire for the night. Cook appeared to be asleep, although he stirred restlessly from time to time.

Ten minutes after Dr Jones had climbed into bed, hoping no doubt for a fairly peaceful night after the stress of the day, the silence was shattered by a shout from Cook, who was sitting bolt upright in bed clutching his stomach in obvious distress. 'Give me the chamber-pot – I am going to be sick!' he gasped. After he had vomited, he sank back weakly. 'Ring the bell and tell the maid to fetch Dr Palmer,' he said.

Dr Jones rang the bell and Elizabeth Mills, who had decided to sit up all night, appeared. She was despatched to fetch Palmer, going herself as the boot-boy was off duty. While she was gone Dr Jones rubbed the back of Cook's neck, where he found 'stiffening of the muscles, a kind of hard feeling'.

In less than three minutes Palmer was in the room, remarking that he had never dressed so quickly in his life, although Elizabeth Mills suspected that he was already dressed when she went to his house, and was to say so later. Palmer gave Cook two pills. No sooner had he swallowed them than he gave a loud shriek, threw himself down on the bed and writhed in convulsions. 'Prop me up or I shall suffocate!' he gasped to Dr Jones. Palmer and Jones tried to do so, but found it impossible as Cook's limbs had gone rigid. Jones also listened to his heart, which he found to be gradually but perceptibly weakening. Jones asked Palmer to fetch some sal volatile to revive him, but by the time he returned with the bottle Cook was at death's door, and less than ten minutes later he was dead. Jones stated quite unequivocally that his death had been due to tetanus (lockjaw).

Dr Bamford was sent for and wrote out a death certificate to this effect, and Palmer asked Elizabeth Mills to arrange for the laying out of the body. While she was still in the room she noticed Palmer searching the pockets of the dead man's clothing, and also looking under the pillows and bolster, not five minutes after the unfortunate man had died, as she was to testify later. She added in her testimony that Cook had always had with him a dark-coloured book with a gold band round the edge, and that he had written something in it on the Monday night before he died. Elizabeth had put the book behind the looking-glass on the dressing-table. 'I have never seen that book since Cook died,' she said. 'I have searched everywhere for it.' This was the book in which Cook recorded all his betting transactions.

The next day Jones left Rugeley, having first written to Cook's stepfather, a man named Stevens, who had last seen his stepson, alive and well, at Euston railway station on his way to the races at Shrewsbury. After Palmer had obtained the death certificate from his dupe Dr Bamford, he went to call on an old school-friend with a document he had drawn up purporting to be an acknowledgement signed by Cook that £4,000 worth of bills had been taken over by him from Palmer. Unfortunately the 'signature' of Cook had not been witnessed, as was necessary in law, and Palmer asked his friend (for a consideration) to sign the document as witness. This, however, was too much even for the friend, who was not averse on occasions to a shady deal or two. 'Good God, man!' he said. 'Cook is *dead*!' Palmer did not press the matter, but went off to order a coffin for the deceased.

Nemesis was, however, creeping nearer, unknown to Palmer, who was supremely confident that he had pulled off yet another 'perfect' murder. Cook's stepfather not only had a great regard for his stepson, but was also fully aware of the large sums of money Cook had won at Shrewsbury, and was anxious to ascertain the whereabouts of this money. Having received news of his stepson's death from Jones on the Wednesday, the following day he went to the lodgings which Cook and Jones had shared to look for a will which he knew his stepson had made some time previously. He found the will, and on the Friday, accompanied by Jones, he went to Rugeley to view the body before the funeral, and met Palmer. He was greatly shocked by the unnaturally stiff appearance of the body, which Jones told him could be ascribed to tetanus. This explanation satisfied Stevens for the time being.

The three of them – Jones, Stevens and Palmer – then went downstairs to hold a discussion in the hotel lounge. Stevens asked Palmer what he knew of his stepson's financial affairs. Palmer replied that there were bills outstanding for £4,000, but Stevens did not believe him. He also asked Palmer what had happened to the two thousand pounds or so which Cook had won at Shrewsbury little more than a week previously. Palmer said that he knew nothing of this, adding, 'If a man dies, then his bets die with him.' Stevens insisted that his stepson would have made a record of his bets in his betting book. Jones and Palmer went up to Cook's room to look for the book, returning shortly afterwards saying that it was nowhere to be found, but that 'no doubt it would soon turn up'.

Stevens appeared, at least for the moment, to accept these glib explanations, and then asked Palmer to take him to an undertaker to arrange for the funeral. To his amazement, Palmer told him that he had already arranged these matters and had ordered an oak coffin. Stevens was not a little put out at Palmer's high-handedness in taking this duty upon himself rather than leaving it to a member of Cook's immediate family, but it seemed there was nothing now he could do about it. He said that he had to return to London, where he lived, in about an hour, and would arrange for Cook to be buried in his mother's grave, as this was what he would have wished, but he said that the body would have to remain at the Talbot Hotel for a day or two while he made the necessary arrangements. Palmer said that this would be all right so long as the coffin was nailed down, and Stevens took his departure. On his way to London he had ample time to brood over Palmer's evasive manner and the suspicions which were growing in his own mind. While in Rugeley he had endeavoured to suppress them, but now, on arrival, he discussed them with various relations, who all agreed that something was not quite right somewhere ...

A post-mortem was ordered, but this was badly bungled and a jar containing the deceased's stomach was dropped – some say that Palmer, who attended the post-mortem, contrived to jog the elbow of an attendant who was carrying it – and when it eventually arrived at the forensic laboratory for examination no poison was found in it apart from a small trace of antimony. Other organs were lost or mislaid, and there was a strong suspicion that Palmer had bribed another attendant to dispose of them, although this could not be proved.

Three days later, on 8 December, Palmer was arrested for the non-payment of the debt to Padwick, and Mrs Palmer, called upon to fulfil her surety and pay the money into court, was horrified to realize that her son had forged her signature to the bills. She refused to pay and informed the court that the bills were forgeries. Enough was enough ...

The inquest into Cook's death was held on 14 December, and after it was brought to light that the two chemists, Roberts and Newton, had supplied Palmer with a number of deadly drugs, and that Cook's betting book –

assiduously looked for by Stevens, who had returned to Rugeley, and which the two chambermaids at the Talbot Hotel remembered had been in Cook's room the night before he died – was missing, feelings in Rugeley began to run very high against Palmer. These revelations, together with his arrest for debt, his forging of his mother's signature, and the extraordinary appearance of Cook's body after death and the equally extraordinary disappearance of vital autopsy tissues, made it inevitable that Palmer would be charged with the murder of Cook. He was held in Stafford Prison.

The people of Rugeley now began to search their memories and put two and two together. There was that affair in the pub when Abley had dropped dead after swallowing a bottle of brandy, supplied by Palmer, for a wager; then there was the death of Mr Bladon, owed £800 by the doctor. Not long afterwards Palmer's wife died and Palmer had come into £13,000 insurance money, and then he had insured his brother Walter, who had quickly died, although the policy money had not been paid. Even babes in arms had not escaped his ministrations if he could thereby evade his financial responsibilities; several of his illegitimate children by various girls had died suddenly, and even four of his wife's children had died before they were a year old, of 'gastric fever', or so it was alleged.

An exhumation order was obtained for the bodies of Palmer's wife Annie and his brother Walter. Both bodies were found by the forensic experts to be permeated with an assortment of deadly drugs. Palmer was now additionally charged with the murder of his wife and his brother by 'the administration of noxious substances with malice aforethought'.

The feelings against Palmer had now reached such a pitch that it would have been impossible to appoint a jury who could have been expected to give him a fair and unbiased trial according to the principles of English law. An application was made to the authorities asking for permission to hold the trial in a different venue, and this was granted, whereby the trial was transferred to the Old Bailey in London. An Act of Parliament was required to enable this to be done, and was passed in time for the trial to begin on 14 May 1856. Ever afterwards this law has been known as 'Palmer's Act' and is now available for other accused against whom there is strong local prejudice. Hardly had Palmer been spirited away from Stafford Prison in the dead of night to London when rumours reached the prison authorities that a plot had been afoot to 'spring' Palmer from gaol and lynch him, a plan instigated, it was thought, by a relative of the hapless Mr Abley. So 'Palmer's Act' came into force only just in time.

The trial took place before the Lord Chief Justice Campbell. The prosecution was led by the Attorney General, Sir Alexander Cockburn, and Palmer was defended by Mr Sarjeant Shee, who conducted his defence with a kind of ferocious desperation, although inevitably doomed to lose his case, despite an eight-hour peroration. The trial lasted twelve days, every one of which saw a packed courtroom, with hundreds more would-be spectators milling around outside, unable to gain admittance. On the last day, 27 May 1856, the jury was out for only one hour before bringing in the expected verdict of guilty of the murder of John Parsons Cook. This was the only murder with which he was charged, the indictments of murdering his wife and his brother being left on file. This was probably because the prosecution's case regarding Cook bristled with witnesses, whereas the past cases would have been much more difficult to prove after the passing of time.

The Prince of Poisoners was returned to Stafford Prison to await his execution, which had been scheduled for 14 June 1856. He was hanged in the courtyard of the prison before 30,000 spectators, many of them having streamed into Stafford from all parts of the country on specially chartered trains. Nearly two dozen platforms were erected to enable the spectators to see over the prison walls into the courtyard, and a guinea per head was charged to secure a vantage-point. Palmer went to his death calmly, and right to the end never made any confession.

Understandably, the people of Rugeley were shamed by the notoriety that Palmer's crimes had brought to their town, and they applied to the Home Secretary for permission to change the town's name. In one account of this action, which may or may not be apocryphal, the Home Secretary is reported to have replied, 'Certainly you may have permission to change the name of your town – I have no objection, provided that you name it after me.'

His name? Lord Palmerston.